WALK
WITH ME,
MY SON

You and I Have Some Stories to Tell

RICHARD ASMET AWID

PROMINENT
BOOKS
EDGE

5830 E 2nd St, Ste 7000 #9983
Casper, WY 82609
USA

Dedication

WALK WITH ME MY SON—
YOU AND I HAVE SOME STORIES TO TELL

is dedicated to the following:

- ❖ my mother, Mary Awid
- ❖ my father, Ahmed Awid
- ❖ my sisters: Lila, Zina, Lily, Emily, Mona, Minnie
- ❖ my brothers: Kemal, Sine, Eddie, Teddy, Jimmy, Mickey, Alex
- ❖ my wife, Soraya Zaki Hafez
- ❖ all of my other relatives including Evelyn and family and members of the Amery families
- ❖ our Lebanese community
- ❖ to all of the friends I have made over the years

Acknowledgement

I wish to acknowledge the receipt of a 2019 Project Accelerator Grant from the Edmonton Heritage Council (EHO), which has financially helped in the publication of this book.

Forward

Welcome to my world! It has taken me approximately two years to gather the information required for the writing of this book.

The book is a historical biographical one and the stories in the book center around the fourteen children and my mother and father who made up our family. The writing of the book was a very tough one for me to write because in addition to the happy stories being told, there are numerous other stories full of sadness. These sad stories were the toughest for me to write and I would be telling you a big lie if I said that no tears came to my eyes as I recalled these stories of sadness.

My stories cover a time period of approximately 135 years and they provide you, the reader, a number of stories not only about my family, but, also, stories about what I refer to as my extended family. You have the opportunity, as you read the book to learn about some of my relatives, the pioneer Lebanese community and members of the public who contributed in great part to the lives my family members, eventually, led.

Some Background Information

My father's name is Ahmed Ali Awid Amerey and I am, Richard Awid, the youngest son in our family. When my father came to Canada, he arrived with the name of Ehmid Alley Awid Amerey. Dad's first name of Ehmid would later have the spelling of Ahmed. How or why this happened, leaves me with no explanation. It also, wasn't a very long time period, after entering Canada that Dad's name would simply become Ahmed Ali Awid. One should note that back in those days, when my father came to the young developing country of Canada, the spellings in the names of people, like my Dad, were often changed by the authorities without the expressed permission of these young immigrants who were very limited in the amount of English that, they could either speak or write.

I, myself, would be born with the name of Asmet Ehmid Alley Awid Amerey where I received my name from my father, Ehmid, my grandfather, Alley and my great grandfather, Awid. Our family's name at that time was Amerey. I note with some interest that my name is similar to Dad's name, in spelling, before he came to Canada.

In my early years of life, a few of my brothers, according to the story that I grew up with, somehow, convinced my Mom and Dad to simply call me Richard Asmet Awid. Notice here how my first name that I was born with, is now my middle name. Furthermore, my family's name became Awid when somewhere along the way, the name Amerey was dropped as the last name. Up to this time, I really have no understanding as to why Amerey was eliminated as the family name.

Keeping in mind, this information about our names, I now want you to know that Dad or Pop, the names I always used for my father and I have a somewhat endless number of interesting stories to tell you about our family. As well, we have an abundance of stories about numerous friends and relatives, who on more than one occasion, played a great part in the life of a very loving family. These friends and relatives really turned our own nuclear family, more often than not, into a family that at times, became quite an enormously large extended family.

Dad was born in the present-day country we now call Lebanon. When he was born, however, Dad lived in the region of the world that was known as the Turkish Ottoman Empire. Within this Empire, there existed another smaller empire, which is known in history, as the Greater Syrian Empire. When the First World War came about in 1914 and ended in 1918, the two empires continued to exist until the time came when changes would occur. By the end of the war, Turkey will have lost its Ottoman Empire as well as the control it had over the Greater Syrian Empire. Over several decades, the victorious nations of the war, would divide the conquered lands into a number of countries that included and became known as the countries of Syria, Iraq and Jordan. Lebanon would become an independent country when it was freed from French domination on November 22nd, 1943. It was in this country that Dad was born in 1882 in a very small village known as Lala. His village would be a distance of about fifty miles (81 kilometres) from Beirut in the direction of the Mediterranean Sea and probably about fifty miles away from present-day Damascus, the capital of Syria in another direction.

My dad's early life, in Lala, was one where he lived with his three brothers Awid, Mohammed and Mahmoud and one sister, Mimoni, along with his father, Alley and his mother, Fatima, who in turn, were my grandparents on my father's side. These were grandparents I never got to see and in all, honesty, I never got to know that much about them. Dad didn't really talk about them that much as I was growing up, but then how much could he really say about his parents when he left home for Canada at the extremely young age of nineteen?

My mother, on the other hand, whose first name was Mary, made her presence into the world in 1895. She was born in the present-day country of Poland, in a region known as Galicia, which at the time of her birth, was part of the Austrian-Hungarian Empire. Her parents, who were my grandparents on Mom's side, brought a very young Mary to Canada when she was only a babe in arms.

As with my father's family, information about my mother's family is also, quite vague. I do, however, know that she had five sisters, and at least one brother, named Pete, who lived in the city of Calgary, roughly about three hundred (300) miles south or 483 kilometres from where we lived in Edmonton. On a number of occasions, some of my family members would travel to Calgary to see Uncle Pete and his wife, Mary, along with their two sons, Bobby and Larry. I was allowed to tag along on several of these trips to Calgary, and I can remember that some of those trips were not the most pleasant for me. I suffered from car sickness, at the time, and I will never forget that whoever was driving the car, in those days, had to stop on numerous occasions because I would be ready to vomit and asked to be let out of the car at various times, so that I could throw up on the roadside instead of inside the car.

My car sickness continued on during the next several trips, to Calgary. This unkind sickness was, eventually, cured when on one occasion, my Aunt Mary told Mom that if she put several pieces of adhesive tape over my belly button, the vomiting would stop. Aunt Mary proved to be a doctor in disguise because Lo! and Behold! my vomiting did honestly, stop on future trips to the land located to the south of our home city, with that adhesive tape placed over my belly button. It was a great relief for me to now be cured from that dreaded car sickness.

What I have presented so far in our story is a little bit of the background which tells you something about the very early years in the lives of my Mom and Dad. Let's now move on to more of our stories as told by my Dad as well as myself.

Dad Leaves Lebanon

Before coming to Canada, Dad told me that he had the responsibility of looking after about one hundred goats that his parents had grazing on their land. In 1901, however, Dad and his friend, Ali Tarrabain, decided that they would like to go to Canada where they figured that they could become rich. So that year, they packed their bags and Dad said good-bye to his father, Alley, and his mother, Fatima. He would, also, bid his good-byes at the same time to his only sister, Mimoni, as well as to his three brothers, Awid, Mohammed and Mahmoud.

Dad and Ali Tarrabain soon made their way from their home village of Lala to Beirut. At this time, Dad never realized that this would be the last time he would ever see his parents and siblings alive. It would be several decades later before Dad returned to Lebanon. In Beirut, the two teenagers would, anxiously, await for the ship that would help move them from Beirut to Canada. After they boarded the ship in Beirut, the ship would then head for Marseilles in France. From France, they moved on to London, England.

While in London, Dad and Ali realized that when purchasing their ship tickets in Beirut, they made a serious mistake. The mistake was one where they actually purchased their tickets to the wrong London. They soon realized that they had purchased their ticket only from Beirut to London, England. In no way did they want their journey to end in London, England. Their journey, in reality, was to land in London, Ontario, Canada. Realizing their mistake, they dug their hands, deep into their pockets and pulled out what money they had left and, at that time, they realized that they had just enough money to buy their tickets to London, Ontario.

After purchasing their tickets for the Canadian London, the ship soon was crossing the Atlantic Ocean and then, in time, it would dock in New York and with a stroke of good luck, they were greeted by an immigration officer who was of Syrian origin and this person was, also, fluent in the Arabic language. The friendly officer told Dad and Ali that they should call themselves by English names because the American

4

authorities were not interested in having Muslims come to the United States. Undoubtedly, this was an early sign of discrimination against Muslims. Dad, taking the Syrian Officer's advice called himself, Charlie. When I asked him why he used the name, Charlie, he said someone in Lala used that name and things worked out quite well for that particular person. Ali Tarrabain, on the other hand, used the English name, Frank. Things must have worked out quite well for Ali and my Dad because within the next twenty-four hours, they were on the train, headed for London, Ontario.

It is now my intention to move on with more stories as told by my Dad and myself. My Dad, as noted earlier left his home village of Lala, in 1901, and also, as noted earlier he was accompanied by his friend, Ali Tarrabain. Both of them were teenagers when they left their homeland. The question that always pops up when I talk about my Dad to my friends is, "Why did he and Ali, along with other Lebanese leave Lebanon?" There probably were several reasons for leaving according to Dad and he seemed to concentrate on the economic factor. He and others thought that they could make a lot of money in Canada. Here, also, are several other reasons as to why numerous teenagers left Lebanon at that time. These people thought that maybe there was a better life in a country such as Canada. It should be noted that Dad could have chosen to go to the United States or a South American country, but he and Ali had their hearts set on reaching Canada.

Another reason as to why the youngsters were leaving their homes is that they were at the age where they were quite adventurous and just wanted to see what other places in the world were like. Also, in those days the Turkish military was losing all kinds of battles that were taking place and there was a fear that with the ongoing loss of numerous lives within the Turkish military there was a very good possibility that the young villagers, such as my Dad, could be forced to serve in the Turkish military. This thought drove fear into people, like my father, and his own parents as well. It didn't make any sense for any of the families to have some of the young villagers serve in a foreign military that was occupying their homeland, and on top of it all, they had thoughts in their mind that they could be shot dead or wounded in any battles that might have taken place.

At times, Dad had a habit of always remembering new things that he said he forgot to mention when he told his stories to me as we walked along the path where he first recalled his stories. On one occasion, Dad brought back the memories when he and Ali Tarrabain packed their bags of belongings and started on their journey to Canada. When telling this story earlier on, Dad forgot to say that his parents knew a few Arabs who were now living in Canada and his parents insisted that he and Ali should make contact with them as soon as possible after the two of them set foot on Canadian territory. It wouldn't be long, however, that the Arabs his parents knew would, themselves, get in touch with the two teenagers. How these Arabs knew that Dad and Ali were now in Canada is a bit surprising, but the fact still remains that Pop and Ali were soon greeted by the Canadian Arabs who would now become their hosts. Dad expressed the view that he and Ali were extremely happy to have these Arabs in their new life in Canada. They would now be cared for while they settled into their new homeland. It is a well-known fact that the Arab culture promotes the caring for each other whether they are related or not. In today's world, however, this caring attitude might not exist in the way it once survived in the years gone by. After telling me this information, Dad had a great big smile on his face and he, gently, laughed and said that he thought this part of his story was now complete.

That same day, Dad wanted to walk a lot and as we walked, more stories poured out of Dad's mind, and for some reason Dad made it clear to me that he was born a Muslim and would always remain a Muslim for the rest of his life, no matter what might happen in the future. When Dad and Ali came to Canada, they would be some of the first Muslims to live in Canada during this time. In all of Canada at this time, there were only a few thousand Muslims.

At the same time, my Dad and Ali left Lebanon, the Christian Arabs, as well, were leaving the Turkish Empire for Canada. When the two groups, Christians and Muslims, came into Canada, they became involved in the world of business. It shouldn't be too hard to understand that the part of the world where these people were leaving was the same area where a group of people, known as the Phoenicians existed for hundreds of years. These Phoenicians became known as the business people of the Middle East. The Phoenicians travelled the Mediterranean and European coastal areas setting up colonies and establishing trade relations with people whose paths they had crossed. People, like my Dad, probably carried with them, this idea of a trading business mentality because of their knowledge about the Phoenicians. Upon the arrival of the newly-landed Muslims and Christians in Canada, most of them couldn't speak much English, if any at all. In nearly all cases, however, they used their ability to communicate by the use of hand and arm gestures. In time, these freshly-minted business people would become known as peddlers in their new land of opportunity.

As they travelled the areas of Canada, some of these peddlers would do quite well in their selling adventures and then they started to be even more adventurous, travelling further and further away from their homebase.

<u>Starting Life in Canada</u>

When it came to following their religion, many of the Christian Arabs found it very easy to get involved in their local Christian communities. These Christian Arabs would be able to attend a number of churches that were already established in the areas in which they were living. In addition, the churches made it possible for these new, young immigrants to learn more English at a faster rate. Furthermore, greater relationships were made possible with other community members who were mainly Christians. The Christian Arabs in time would open some garment factories and started to manufacture items such as shirts, pants and boots.

The Christian Arabs, generally, maintained a strong relationship with the Muslim immigrants because they understood in those days that they all belonged to a very proud Arab culture. Over the years, however, some conflicts would result between a limited number of Christians and Muslims when different groups started to come to Canada from Lebanon. Those having their differences probably brought some of the Middle Eastern beliefs they grew up with into their Canadian lifestyle. Overall, however, Christian and Muslim Arabs got along very well in the Canada of the past as well as the Canada we live in today, whether it's at a business level and/or on a social level. Before moving westward, the Christian Arabs would establish themselves in various towns and villages located in Quebec, Ontario and the Maritimes.

The Muslims on the Move

The Muslims, like my Dad, Ehmid, settled first of all in the communities of Ontario, but in time, the desire to move westward became part of their lives. They noticed that a few of their friends had, previously, made their way to Western Canada, and once there, they realized the great opportunities they could take advantage of. The land, for example, could be bought for a very cheap price and farms, although limited in numbers, had people living on them who could buy supplies they were selling as peddlers and that meant money could be made in this area if the immigrant Arab showed the desire to work hard in order to achieve a higher level of life. This is how my Dad's working life got started in Canada.

As mentioned before, Dad was only nineteen years old when he came to Canada. He passed his medical examination upon entry into the country, and was allowed to remain in Canada as a landed immigrant. Some other Arabs, however, were not as lucky as Dad. These unlucky ones failed their medicals, and at that point they were only given two choices as to what was to happen to them. Either they could return to their country of origin or they could go to a South American country. A number from this group chose South America because they would be able to join other Arabs who had taken up residency there. In some cases, when two brothers came to Canada, one brother would pass his medical and was allowed to stay in Canada while the other brother who was unable to pass the medical exam, decided to go to South America. Some brothers, in situations like this, might never see each other again or it could be numerous years before they would, eventually, meet up again with their siblings, who had been separated for so many years. Sad, as the situation may have been, this is the way life was in those days.

Dad Moves Westward

Dad's life in Eastern Canada went quite well but he made a decision that he should move westward because some of his friends had moved to the west during the past several months. He made his way from London, Ontario into Manitoba. Upon his arrival in Manitoba, he chose to settle in Winnipeg. I am not certain how many Arabs were living in Winnipeg when he arrived there, but as he told me this part of his story, he insisted that there were some Arabs there, but their numbers probably were limited.

In Winnipeg, Dad began his western peddler way of life. When living in London, Ontario, Dad, also, worked as a peddler. No matter where my Dad started his peddler life, he would always start that life by buying a few suitcases that he could either strap to his back and/or carry the case or cases in his hands. He led this type of life for several years and he would quite often travel back and forth from Winnipeg to Brandon, a city not that far from Winnipeg. In time he would be joined by other Arab peddlers, such as his cousin, Sam Esmeil Jamha and his nephew, Alex Amery. Dad was the person who supported Sam and Alex in their move to Canada. The three of them would be joined in the next few years by members from the Tarrabain and Ganam families. This group of peddlers, although few in numbers, had a drive within them which gave them the desire to be very ambitious in order to improve their everyday way of life. The life of the peddler, in many cases, proved to be extremely interesting where they travelled a lot and met many different people.

The Life as a Peddler

What made the peddler's lives interesting, started off with the suitcases they had to purchase. Having little money, the peddler had to bargain with the owners of the cases for the best prices possible. The best price generally, meant that the peddler was looking for the lowest price to pay for any of the suitcases purchased. Each peddler would use his Middle Eastern bargaining skills to get the cheapest price that was available. The peddlers, needless to say, did very well in their bargaining endeavours and maybe, as well, their lack of fluent English made the seller of the cases feel sorry for them. Also, we can't rule out the fact that possibly the suitcase seller just wanted to help people out and, thus, offered an excellent price for a suitcase.

After purchasing their cases, the peddlers would fill at least one suitcase with supplies such as beads, handkerchiefs, scarves and maybe some shirts and pants. These peddlers would purchase their goods either from suppliers in Winnipeg, which was a big manufacturing centre at the time and/or they would bring in their supplies from eastern Canada, especially from Toronto and Montreal. The suppliers from eastern Canada, were, usually, in this early time period, Arab suppliers who had opened their factories one by one over several years after coming to Canada. These Arabs were, more likely than not, Christian Arabs who had an excellent relationship with the Arabs of Western Canada. As previously stated, it is the Arab culture that helped to bind the good relationship between these early Arab Christians and Muslim pioneers. The two groups in these early years believed that their relationship could grow very strong with effort on the part of both groups. Unfriendly situations for the early pioneer peddlers really did not exist that much during most of their every day way of life.

The Peddlers Go on the Road

The peddler, with his cases, now fully loaded, during those early days would attach one case onto his back and if he had a second case, would carry it, gripped by his hand. He would then start to walk from house to house, or farm to farm as well as village to village where he always tried to sell his goods loaded in those suitcases whose weights were equal to or even more than the peddler's own weight. These young, early salesmen (as they would later be called), realized that the more they sold, the lighter the cases would become. In addition, they were now earning money by selling their goods. For most of the peddlers, the money they were now earning could purchase more goods but some of them thought that the earnings could increase if their English language skills were improved. Up to this time, in their sales pitches, they used their limited English, along with hand gestures and movements of the arms to persuade the customer to make a purchase. While using these techniques in their sales pitch, they were able to get their selling points across to their customers. So the peddlers went about improving their skills in English with the help of others along with their own desire to improve those same skills.

It wasn't long before the peddler's sales began to grow and, at the same time, their English skills improved, as well. In addition, the peddlers made new friends on their journeys as they sold their numerous supplies.

On a number of occasions, the customers would invite the peddlers to sleep overnight in order to get some well-deserved rest before journeying on the next day. Many invitations of sleeping overnight were extended by people who lived on the farms as well as those who lived in the towns and villages. There was little, if any discrimination, against the peddlers as far as Dad could remember for that time period. The time we are talking about are the years between 1902 and 1914. In 1914, World War I began and some changes started to come about as to how certain people (European mainly) behaved towards "different others" such as the Arabs.

The year, 1914, would see the start of a much larger war than previous wars had been. In this war, the Ottoman Empire would side with the enemy forces. This knowledge of siding with the so-called enemy side would soon reach the shores of Canada and it wouldn't be long before the Arabs, in general, would be labelled as the dirty Turks. There is really no doubt that discrimination against the Arabs started to show its ugly face at this time. Thus life for many of these people became a little tougher to live. Some of these Arabs decided to return to the Middle East while others decided to stick it out in their new Canadian homeland. Immigration to Canada from the Arab World virtually came to a halt. Those Arabs remaining in Canada, in some cases, started to grow fearful of what might take place as the days and months moved on. Some of these Canadian Arabs, became so fearful that they, too, decided to return to their homeland, My own father gave much thought about going back to his village of Lala. Dad, however, decided to remain in Canada and continued on with the life he had begun to establish in his new adopted land. He believed, at the time, that there was something inside of him, which told the young Ehmid that he should stay in Canada rather than leave the country. Over the next number of weeks, my Dad, Ehmid, would continue to peddle his supplies. His sales tended to increase and as a result these sales allowed him to earn more money. In his storytelling, Pop never talked about being discriminated against, in any way that he could remember.

Dad Meets Mom

In 1915, Dad opened a general store in Brandon, Manitoba. This store allowed him to carry a big supply of merchandise. The peddlers who had been around for a number of years would go to his store and purchase a lot of their supplies from him. One of the employees he would hire to help run the store was his future wife and my mother, Mary. Mom was younger than Dad, but in time a very loving relationship would be established between the two of them. Wedding bells soon would be ringing and Ehmid and Mary would in the following days become known as Mr. and Mrs. Ehmid Awid. After their marriage took place, Dad continued to look after the store and my mother would help out as much as she could. Her help, in time, would become more limited because she was now expecting their first child. Born, in 1916, Alex would now become the first born of the Awid family. Fifteen others would be born into our family. Unfortunately, two members of the family would die before they reached the age of two. Of the fourteen family members that survived, there would be six girls and eight boys.

The names of the girls would be Fatima who was named after Dad's mother and who would become known as Minnie, in English. The next four girls would be called Mimoni (Mona in English), Amne with the English name of Emily, Mariam whose English name was Lily and Zinab, who was named Zina in English. The youngest daughter born was Lila and this was her name in both Arabic and English.

The eight brothers were with the English names in brackets; Ali (Alex), Awid (Mickey), Mahmoud (Jim), Ehmid (Ed or Eddie), Mohammed (Ted or Teddy) who were twins, Sine, known by this name in both Arabic and English, Kemal (Ken), and myself, Asmet who would have the English name of Richard. My Arabic name, Asmet, is a result of being named after a famous Turkish Prime Minister, Ismet Inonu and my brother, Kemal, would be named after a great President of Turkey called Kemal Ataturk. My father seemed to have liked these two Turkish leaders quite a bit and this, undoubtedly, gave him enough reason for my parents to name Kemal and myself after these individuals. Note how my name is going to be spelled with a capital "A" rather than a capital, "I".

The first several members of the family were born in Brandon, Manitoba while the rest of the family would have their births take place in Edmonton, Alberta. When my parents moved to Edmonton from Brandon, in 1928, around July 15th of that year, they brought several children with them. The children were Alex, Minnie, Mona, Emily, Mickey and Lily. The seventh child, Zina, was still in the stage of being carried by Mother. At this point, I want to emphasize that before moving from Brandon, Dad journeyed by train to Edmonton by himself several months before the move took place in order for him to be sure that Edmonton was the suitable location that he wanted it to be.

The Move Comes

Dad soon returned to Brandon and told Mom that things looked pretty good in Edmonton. He, then, had a long talk with Mom and said to her, "Let's move to Edmonton!" Mom agreed to the move, even though it meant leaving her parents behind, and soon they were ready to leave Brandon for Edmonton.

Upon arriving in Edmonton, my mother and father were greeted by a number of people from the Lebanese community. Cousin Sam Jamha was there along with Ali Hamdon, Alex Hamilton and George Seede. Kalil Rahall and his brother, Mahmoud Rahall were, also, there to greet my parents, along with Jim Darwish and Peter Baker. Dad felt that it was an honour to have so many of the community come and greet them.

Upon those early arrival days, in their new city, Dad's memory, during our walks, quite often journeyed back to Brandon. When he and his fellow Lebanese, met over coffee, Dad told the gathered group one day that from 1916 to 1928, he operated his general store many hours each day in Brandon. My father boasted on one occasion during that time period of 1916 to 1928, his customers considered him as a very fair-minded person and it, certainly, wasn't hard for him to make friends with just about anyone. Dad believed that success in the business world would only be possible if you treated your customers with kindness, and a good understanding of the customer he was dealing with. While running his business, Pop would often give a line of credit to a number of his customers, if these customers were in a real serious bind. In addition, he would offer these people all kinds of help whenever he knew that his customers, as well as his friends, required the assistance. Also, my father being the generous person that he was, often made sure that he would send some money back to Lala, his birth town, in Lebanon. This money being sent back to Lala was meant to help out his relatives who quite often needed that help. Dad would continue to send money to Lala for many years throughout his entire lifetime. When Mom and Dad moved to Edmonton, Dad would continue to hold meetings at his stores and he always insisted that as long as he had a store, that store would always be a gathering place for the Lebanese who were arriving from the Middle East and other parts of Canada. Dad realized that a number of these newcomers would soon become the new peddlers who either bought supplies from Dad or got the merchandise on credit. Just like the earlier peddlers, these newcomers would have their suitcases available and they loaded them up with goods and then they would take off to the farms, towns, villages and even other cities where they tried to sell their goods. In a realistic way, Dad was of the firm belief that many of these newcomers would be reliving the days when people, such as Dad, himself, started their own peddling adventures. These meetings, with his Lebanese friends continued on for a long time during those early Edmonton days.

Life in Edmonton Begins

When Dad and Mom settled in their new city, Pop opened a general store located in the downtown area of the city. This general store had no groceries or hardware supplies. His main merchandise was mainly clothing which he knew that the peddlers would want. Dad stayed at the location of his first store for about one year and then moved to another location on Jasper Avenue and 97 Street. This location proved to be very poor for business and, once again, he decided to move because of the poor sales as well as a very high cost for rent. So Dad was on the move again in his search for a suitable location. This time, he opened another general store about four blocks north from the previous location. Business at this new location started to pick up and Dad would keep this store opened for approximately three years. Over the next several years, Pop kept opening and closing stores as he dealt with those awful depression years which everybody had to now live with.

Even though the times continued to be tough for Dad, he remained in the store business until 1945. He, then, sold whatever supplies he had to a Jewish friend called Hymie Weisler. The amount of money he got for his goods was quite small in size. Dad then made the decision to talk to some big suppliers and began working on getting as many bargains as he could from these suppliers. In order to buy these bargains, he acquired a loan from Weisler and then he bought the goods which were resold to a number of merchants as well as some storekeepers. Dad did this type of work for several of the following years and, then, he finally made the decision to retire from the world of business.

While in the business world one of Dad's biggest suppliers was a company known as G.W.G. which was the shortened form for the company called the Great Western Garment. From this company, when Dad started to deal with it, in the 1920s decade, he bought all kinds of shirts that were being sold for around $12.00 a dozen. As well, Pop would buy some groceries such as crushed wheat for nine cents a pound, along with chickpeas for twelve cents a pound. These groceries were bought from a wholesale grocer in Montreal which was named Aboosamra Kouri. He bought socks for $1.90 a dozen and handkerchiefs for eighty-eight cents a dozen. Buster Brown socks were bought for $4.50 a dozen. These supplies were bought from a wholesale in Winnipeg called Sure Brothers Limited. Further purchases took place when Dad bought suitcases from the Western Suitcase Manufacturing Co. in Winnipeg. Twenty-four inch suitcases were bought by Dad for $1.20 each and the twenty-six inch suitcase was bought for $1.25 each.

When buying his supplies for the store, Dad, always, would look for the best deals from the suppliers and if he felt that he didn't get that deal, he soon would have a letter going to the offices of those businesses. When the letters were going to be sent out to the suppliers, Dad knew that he was unable to write them, himself, so he got someone else to help him draft and write the letters and usually that helper would be the one who typed or wrote the letters. Of course, it would cost Dad some money and/or goods to get the letters written and mailed out.

In addition to buying his store's supplies, Dad was responsible for supplying the money needed to pay the utilities bills as well as paying the grocery costs for a family that grew in numbers every year or two. My father had to work very hard to make sure that the money supply kept coming in.

When doing his storytelling, Dad seemed to relate to me that during the time period from 1920 to 1926, that not much new was happening businesswise. The older peddlers, who started buying from Dad a number of years before, kept coming for their supplies and some of them still continued to ask for credit while others paid for their purchases either by cash or cheque. The new peddlers, also, kept coming to the area where Dad's store was and, as a result, Dad's general store continued to remain as a well-respected supply centre of goods for many of these peddlers.

Undoubtedly, one of Dad's favourite suppliers was the Great Western Garment Company, also known as G.W.G. Pop realized that this company had excellent products which were well-designed as well as well-made. The company's products had a very long-life for items like shirts, pants, and especially their famous outstanding cowboy jeans.

Dad sold many items manufactured by G.W.G. and the costs for the merchandise was very inexpensive for the quality of the merchandise a customer was receiving. The items, my father purchased, along with their costs, were documented in the numerous business books Dad kept in order to keep better track of his business dealings. For some reason or reasons many of Dad's record books were saved by some of our family members and these books were, eventually, moved into the basement of the house, my two older brothers, Alex and Mickey, had built for Mom, Dad and the family members who were still living at home. When I look back at this time period which made it possible for me to examine a number of these books, I now, realize how important, historically, these books are as a part of our family's story as well as how valuable they are to the partial early history of the Lebanese people in Canada.

Dad Recalls More Stories

One day, Dad and I left the house so that we could tell more stories to each other. On this day, he started with a story by saying he and Mom remained in Brandon for their early married years because it was here that so many great things happened. As stated earlier, my parents were married in Brandon and several of the older family members were born there. Brandon was, also, the place where many friendships had been established over numerous years and Brandon was the center that made it possible for my Dad to help out his peddler friends by supplying them with the goods they would require in order to make a living in a rather very young Western Canada.

During this time, from the start of the 1920's to a year or two beyond the mid-point of that decade, Mom, Dad and the children of the family seemed to have led an enjoyable life, as far as I know. One thing, however, started to play in their minds when they realized that several of their Lebanese friends started to leave Manitoba and headed further west. Their friends began to settle in Saskatchewan and Alberta which both joined the Dominion of Canada in 1905.

These two provinces were relatively young at this time and probably the friends who had moved westward may have had the feeling that opportunities galore existed in these two new provinces. My parents heard stories that some of their Lebanese friends bought farms and became the farmers of the land. Others, who could afford it, became big store suppliers for anyone who would do business with them. These Lebanese invested their money in the warehouse business where they had tremendous supplies of goods located throughout the warehouse. The Tarrabain brothers, Ali, who came to Canada in 1901 with Dad, and Mahmoud, for example, were two of the Lebanese who had a warehouse business in Edmonton which was loaded with supplies that ran into many thousands of dollars for that time period.

Another group, small as it was, became a group of fur traders. This particular group of Lebanese pioneers learned most of their beginning fur-trading skills from the indigenous people who lived in the areas where the Lebanese went to do business. The Lebanese are, in general, very sociable people and found it quite easy to establish a relationship with the natives. Numerous Lebanese, in order to further their friendship with the indigenous people, even learned to speak the language of these people that they were doing business with. Some Lebanese would, in time, marry women from the indigenous community.

In Saskatchewan, the Lebanese would settle mainly in the smaller communities found throughout the southern parts of Saskatchewan. Dad, however, had a cousin who settled in Prince Albert. His name was Frank Amery, but in Prince Albert, he would become known as Frank Almer. I and the rest of our family had the opportunity to meet and talk to Frank and his wife, Nellie, whenever they came to Edmonton. They visited Edmonton on a number of occasions and stayed at our house during those visits. Frank, in my opinion, was a very amazing person. He was a little guy and, perhaps, a little bit on the short side, but he always had a good hearty laugh and had a great smile that no money could ever buy. Frank Almer was a man who carried some special form of magic in his body. He had the magical ability to find missing people. At times, police forces in both Canada and the United States would call upon him to help find these missing people. As reported in numerous newspaper articles, stories about his special ability were written up in these newspapers found throughout parts of North America. The news reports always told how Frank directed the police to specific locations where the missing people could be found. One newspaper article from an Edmonton newspaper in the 1940's said that "some years ago, three men and a woman disappeared in Prince Albert." Frank Almer was called upon by the police to work on the case. It was wintertime when Frank received the call. Frank told the police that it would be wise to wait until the break-up came in the spring in order to conduct the search. When the search got started, Frank Almer ordered the searching parties to drag a spot in a lake in the Prince Albert National Park and it was there that the bodies were recovered.

When Frank visited Edmonton, one time, he was asked by the city police to find a missing person. The psychic, Frank, told the police that if they go four miles downstream from the High Level Bridge, they will find the body of a citizen on the north bank of the river. The body was found after the man was missing for several months.

Cousin Frank, also, claimed that when several hundred families in the Prince Albert area failed to find water after drilling many wells, they called upon him and, in addition, to finding the wet spots for them, he foretold just how far the drills would have to penetrate before water would gush up in the holes.

I, personally, remember when Frank and his wife, Nellie, visited Edmonton many years ago. I was only a youngster during this visit, probably only in my early teens. During that visit, I asked Cousin Frank how he was able to find the missing people. At this point, he looked at me and squeezed his fingers together and said the words, "piggy, piggy!". He, of course, was playing a joke on me by saying these words. It wasn't long, however, before Frank got serious and he then told me, in the most serious way, it was the power of God that gave him his ability to figure out where the missing people and water could be found. Although he didn't find all of the people, he was asked to find, his percentage rating of successful finds was very high, indeed.

When Cousin Frank Almer passed away in Prince Albert, it was a snowy, October day, in Edmonton. My father and one of my older brothers, Mickey, would drive to Prince Albert for the funeral. As for me, I would remain at home in order to attend my university classes. Upon Frank's passing, tears came to my eyes and I realized with weighted sadness that our extended family now must cope with the loss of this beloved cousin of ours.

Over the following years, after Frank's death, his wife, Nellie, would come to visit us in Edmonton. She always treated me with the greatest respect and with a kindness a loving mother would show to her own son. At times the children from Frank and Nellie's family, also came and visited us—especially, the two daughters, Pearl and Ruth. Pearl would in time move to Edmonton where she passed away around 2013. She lived to be about ninety years of age. Pearl always kept a close family connection with our family over the years.

As I recall the memories I have of Frank, Nellie, and their family by writing this information, I think how blessed I was to have them be part of my life. Their closeness of family life brought our families together for many happy and enjoyable time periods in the past.

Michael Alley Haynee and Edward Nasserden

On another day, my Dad continued to tell me more stories, stories which never seemed to have an end to them. My Dad always did have a great memory and after telling me so much about his cousin Frank Almer, he once again, went back to the time when he and the rest of the family were moving from Brandon to Edmonton. He remembered stopping in Regina on that trip when the family met up with an old Lebanese friend by name of Michael Alley Haynee.

Dad then started to recall information about Mr. Haynee. Haynee was born in Beirut in 1874 but at that time he had the name of Mohammed Ali Ta Haynee. When Haynee left the Middle East, he went to North Dakota in 1899 and, eventually, moved to Regina in 1903. He, thus, became known as Regina's first Muslim. When he reached Regina, Haynee anglicized his name to Michael Alley Haynee. Within a short time, he would open a business known as Alley's Warehouse and Retail Dry Goods on the corner of Winnipeg Street and 12th Avenue. His business, also, operated pushcarts that went from community to community in Southern Saskatchewan.

Michael Haynee knew many languages and he served as a translator for the Northwest Mounted Police as well as for the new immigrants who had made their way to Regina. Michael then returned to his homeland of Lebanon in 1911. Upon his return to Canada, he would bring a bride with him. The bride, whose name was Irene Ganam, was a sister of a friend in Regina. Haynee was forty-seven when he married and the marriage resulted in ten daughters and seven sons being born.

Michael Alley Haynee died on May 26th, 1982 at the grand-old age of 108. When he died, it seemed likely that Haynee was probably the oldest person in Regina and possibly the oldest person in all of Saskatchewan.

The city of Regina, honoured Michael Haynee by naming a street after him in Regina and today it is still known as Haynee Street. His store was declared as a heritage store, but, unfortunately, the store no longer exists today.

In addition to meeting Michael and Irene on this stopover to Edmonton, the Haynee family had a friend drop by while Mom and Dad were visiting. My Dad didn't know this Lebanese man other than his last name was Nasserden who, also, came to Canada a number of years before.

It seems as if Dad brought Nasserden's name into his story because this Nasserden had a son by the name of Edward. Edward was born in 1919 at a place called Clark's Crossing, Saskatchewan. He died in 1995. What Dad found of real interest was that Edward Nasserden served as a Progressive Conservative member of Parliament for the constituency in Saskatchewan known as Rosthern. Edward was first elected to office in 1958 and re-elected in 1962, 1963 and 1965. He was defeated as a Member of Parliament in 1968. Dad took great pride in knowing that his fellow-countrymen from Lebanon or their family members could rise to the position of an elected member of Canada's Parliament centered in Ottawa, Ontario.

After telling me the information about Michael Haynee and Edward Nasserden, Dad went back to the time when our family came to Edmonton. He recalled how the family came from Regina to Edmonton by train and how they were greeted by members of the Lebanese community. Dad said that he would always remember how the community members helped him with the openings of his stores and how the community members were always there if Mom and Dad required their assistance.

Uncle Sam Jamha and Alex Amery

Dad then said that two of his favourite people in Edmonton, in addition to numerous others, were two of his relatives who moved to Edmonton several years ago and then made Edmonton, at the time, a type of permanent residency.

Those two relatives that Dad would speak of, often, were Esmeil Sam Jamha and Alex Amery. Quite often whenever I saw Sam, I would call him Uncle Sam. Alex Amery, on the other hand, became known to me as Cousin Alex. All of these Lebanese friends and relatives loved to visit with each other and while visiting they could always recall, during any conversations, their lives in Lebanon and the relatives and friends they had left behind. In addition, they would spend time telling stories about how their new lives began in Canada, along with the successes and failures they had experienced while living here up to that time. Their stories always told about the good times as well as the tough times.

Sam Jamha spent much of his early life as a peddler, but as he grew older, he went into the furtrading business. As a furtrader, Sam would travel throughout Alberta and probably into Saskatchewan in order to either trap the fur-bearing animals, himself, and/or he would buy huge amounts of furs from the native people. In dealing with the natives, Sam acquired some of the native language, knowing full well that he could deal with people in a much better way by communicating with them in their language. This type of thinking on Sam's part was absolutely right because Sam quite often, would return to Edmonton with loads of furs. He would then sell a lot of these furs to the Jewish fur buyers who had their businesses located along a few of the major streets in Edmonton.

In addition to his business ties, Sam settled down and married a beautiful English lady by the name of Vera Jowett. They were married in 1922. I always referred to Vera as my Aunt Vera. Whenever Aunt Vera and Uncle Sam went to weddings, they quite often were the star attractions who would dance the nights away on many of these occasions. The couple proved to be exceptional dancers who could dance around the floor with the greatest of ease and exceptional graceful movements. They both loved the movements of the dances they were involved with.

Sam and Vera had two sons, Roy and Bobby, and one daughter named Mariam. Roy was probably the most successful of the family members. He became the Chairman of the Workmen's Compensation Board, at one point, and as well he was the President of the Alberta Federation of Labour. In addition, Roy Jamha was one of the founding members of the political party, NDP, in 1961.

Sam's health was not always in good shape. One of the reasons his health started to fail him is that he was a very heavy cigarette smoker. His lungs became affected in a very serious way. Eventually, he was admitted to the hospital and past away from a smoking disease. His wife, Vera, continued to live for a number of years after Sam had died.

My Uncle Sam Jamha would be honoured in the city of Edmonton by having the road called Jamha Road named after him. This honour, in my opinion, speaks highly of this man who came to Canada at a young age and who knew very little English, at the time and, yet, he had that determined desire to succeed with his new life. The life, he led, made Uncle Sam a very important part of the Lebanese community as well as a great character who played his part in helping to shape a bit of Canada as we know it today. Uncle Sam Jamha passed away in 1974.

There is one other story that I personally want to tell about Sam and his fellow Lebanese friends and relatives. The story goes like this. The main day of prayers for the Muslims is Friday. Sam and his friends were very devout prayer-goers who went to the Al Rashid Mosque every Friday, unless one of them got sick. Each Friday, after the prayers were completed, Sam, Alex Darwish and Mike Tarrabain would be brought to our house, by my brother, Mickey, who, also attended the mosque for prayer services along with the previous mentioned individuals. My Mom would always have a big lunch ready for them upon their arrival. They, indeed, seemed to enjoy their lunch and, at the same time, had many interesting conversations. When everything was completed in the kitchen, except for the washing of the dishes, Dad and his group would slowly make their way to the living room where they gathered around a small round table that was always located by Dad's semi-big armchair. At this point each of these gentlemen would place themselves around that table and they would now get ready for a long afternoon of card games. While they were doing this, Mickey would let them know that he had to get back to work because it was getting on to 2:00 P.M. Mickey then left the house.

Dad and his group got ready for the first card game. This card game, along with the rest of the card games played on those Friday afternoons, would have the winner of the game, become the owner of twenty-five cents (25¢) from each of the three losing players. The winner for each of the games would receive the grand amount of seventy-five cents. That seems to have been big money in those days.

Sometimes these games would go on for hours and probably the greatest amount ever won on one of those days was in the $2.00 to $3.00 range. On a number of occasions, numerous games would have the individuals yelling at each other thinking that one of the players was possibly cheating—not really in a mean way but in a rather, what I would call, friendly manner.

Most of the time, the card players would keep the games going until supper time. Their supper, of course, was made by Mom. Usually, the cardplayers finished the supper with a cup or two of coffee. They, then, returned to the cardplaying and would, eventually, call it an evening around 9:00 P.M., when Mike and Alex both said it was time for them to go home. Sam, on the other hand, would stay behind and talk to Dad. At about 10:30 P.M., I would drive Sam to the bus stop located in the downtown area so that he could catch his bus home.

There are undoubtedly, other stories that I could tell about my Uncle Sam, but those stories will just have to wait for another time.

On another occasion, Dad started to tell me another story and this time the story was about our cousin, Alex Amery. There is no doubt in my mind that Cousin Alex was a real comical character who could lose his temper at times, but when his bad temper came about, the most damage he would do is just raise his voice and then he would continue on talking in a very normal manner. Overall, Alex Amery was always a very kind-hearted person.

Whenever Cousin Alex told stories, he would quite often have great humour in those stories and, as well, each story seems to have had a number of swear words in them. Those of us who were fortunate enough to listen to his stories would laugh quite often as the stories were being told.

Alex Amery was one of the original Lebanese peddlers who went out selling his goods by horse and wagon. He spent a lot of time, over the warmer months of the year, in a location known as Rimbey, Alberta. Because of his likable personality, he developed many long-lasting friendly relationships with his customers. When winter started to settle in, Alex would stop selling the goods he still had. He made certain that he left his horses, wagon and supplies in good hands over those winter months.

As the weather turned colder, my cousin Alex made his way to Edmonton and spent the next several winter months at our house. When Alex came to stay with us during those colder months of the year, he would always bring my parents two frozen turkeys with their heads still on, but those dead birds always had their heads wrapped with a brown piece of paper. Each of those frozen birds, when stretched out, would probably be a little longer than a metre in length. My mom would cook one of the turkeys for the Christmas dinner and the second turkey would be used for the New Year's dinner gathering. When Alex brought the turkeys to our house, Mom always stored them in the porch attached to our house. It seems to me, as I recall that during the time the two turkeys were being kept in that porch, the weather was cold enough that the turkeys had no chance, whatsoever, to perform a thawing ritual.

The two turkey dinners made it possible for two great family gatherings each year where the married family members in addition to the still-single family members gathered around Mom and Dad where they expressed their pleasure in these memorable events taking place. If any children were born at the time, they, of course, came to each gathering. There is no doubt, in my own mind, that these gatherings always brought our family members much closer together.

Alex Amery, quite often, at these suppers was the center of attention and he always told us a number of surprising things. One of the interesting things he would tell us was that he only went to school for one day. During that day, however, Alex claimed that he learned twenty-seven languages. No one, who was present at the gathering, could prove if the words Alex said were actually words from the languages he insisted he learned while at school that one day. We tended to play along with Alex by believing that he really did know many words from many languages. We, of course, spoke mainly English at home while Dad and Alex spoke Arabic and Mom spoke Ukrainian. Growing up, Mom and Dad felt that it was best for the family members to know English because it would be a lot easier for us to get along in the Canadian society we were now being raised in. When I look back at this situation, I now can only wish that

Dad would have taught us Arabic and that Mom would have taught us the Ukrainian language. Dad's birth language of Arabic could always be heard in the house when the Lebanese friends came to visit.

In addition to his language skills, Cousin Alex, at times, would pick up the back of a wooden chair with only his teeth. Also, with his teeth, he could remove a bottle cap without any problem from a soft drink bottle. At our gatherings, as well, Alex became famous for his sayings such as calling someone in his stories, a dirty skunk or he referred to some people as dirty "bicks" which in everyday language would mean dirty bitches. One of his famous sayings, when he wanted to insult someone was to say that the person was a big shot from a small town. These days, really were the good, old days, where you had a chance to see in action and hear in words, a person like my Cousin Alex. When the winter months came to an end, Alex would bid goodbye to our family and return to his peddling way of life once again.

Alex Amery would live into his eighties and up to the time of his retirement, he operated a few grocery stores along with the help of his wife and children. The stores would be opened for many hours each day, seven days a week.

The back part of each of Alex's stores would serve as a social gathering area for the many friends who would come and visit the family. The gatherings, once again, in my opinion proved how sociable those early pioneer Arabs were in their behavior and they showed great cleverness in how they made it possible to pass their socialization skills on to the members of their own family. Even though Alex and his wife, Khadija were not educated in a formal school setting, they made sure that their children received the best education possible. One of the sons, Mahmoud, would graduate from university and became a teacher. Awid, the oldest son, became an accountant and Ahmed, Mohammed and Mariam made their way into the business world.

Alex Amery passed away in 1999 and his wife, Khadija, after suffering from numerous poor health problems passed away in early 2018.

In addition to relatives like Sam Jamha and Alex Amery who provided many hours of contact with our family members, there were lots of friends who came through the doors of our house over the years.

When I talked to Dad about these friends, there certainly was no shortage of names that came out of Dad's mouth. As we journeyed on with our walk one day, Dad recalled the visits to our house of people like Najeebie Houssian.

Dad's Stories Continue

Najeebie Houssian spent many years in a place called Ceylon, Saskatchewan. The family operated several stores and, eventually, moved to Grande Prairie, Alberta. When Najeebie passed away, she was 102 years old.

Dad then mentioned the name of Alex Walfe who was one of the smartest dressers around and worked as a waiter. As a youngster, I remember him coming to the house smoking a cigarette which was always held in a holder entrenched in his mouth. Other names come into Dad's stories including people like Alex Kutney, John Lulu, Pete Blonde, Ameen "King" Ganam, Jim Darwish, Ali Hamdon and Mahmoud Tarrabain. Dad would have a few things to say about each one and on several occasions he would have a lot more to say about some of the people more than others. Pop would recount stories that were strictly dedicated to friendship, while other stories were more business-oriented. Several of the stories might even deal with both a social content to them along with business matters thrown in as well.

As a youngster, I remember, when Alex Kutney came to visit us at home. He would always bring a very small individual water pipe with him and while he got himself into a comfortable position, in the house, during his visit, he would get his water pipe going and today I can still hear the water bubbles coming from that water pipe of his. After remaining in Edmonton for a number of years, Alex Kutney would return to his home village in Lebanon where he passed away.

John Lulu was another interesting character in our family's life. I can't swear for certain if he was of Lebanese origin, but I can, positively, say that he came to visit Mom and Dad on a regular basis. John was a person who had some severe medical problems and had a lot of work done on his heart. Although sick on numerous occasions, John Lulu would survive to a good old age.

During his healthier days, John lived the life of a peddler and he would travel many times, by car, into areas of both Alberta and Saskatchewan selling his supply of merchandise. Meadow Lake, Saskatchewan was one of his favorite places to visit.

Pete Blonde was my Mom's brother. I remember him very well when we went for visits to Calgary. My Uncle Pete was a very kind person and when we were visiting with him and his wife, Mary, we were always welcomed into their home with open arms. Aunt Mary has been mentioned earlier in my writing, when I said she was the one who provided a cure for my car sickness.

Ameen "King" Ganam came to visit us with his father, Sied Ameen Ganam Kadri. Sied was one of the original Lebanese pioneers who came to Canada in the same time period as my Dad did. Ameen "King" Ganam was one of three children in the Ganam family. The other two children were Lila and Saleem. Lila became a teacher after graduating from university and her extensive studies at university made it possible for her to become known as Dr. Lila Fahlman. She married Al Fahlman. Dr. Lila Fahlman is given credit for starting the organization known as the Canadian Council of Muslim Women and, today, this organization is found in a number of cities across Canada. Dr. Lila has been honoured with an Order of Canada award and, in addition, she has an Edmonton Public School named after her.

Saleem, on the other hand, was a very religious person and he became involved in the interfaith area where he promoted an understanding of the religion of Islam. He, also, wrote numerous books on this religion. Saleem was married to his wife, Mary, for many years and the marriage only ended when Saleem passed away while he was in his early nineties. Mary died several years after Saleem.

At this point, Dad and I recalled some of the life of Ameen "King" Ganam. Ameen's father had no doubt that this son was very musically inclined from an extremely young age. At the beginning of his teenage years, Ameen took a very great interest in wanting to play the fiddle.

His fiddle interest probably started when he heard someone at a musical performance or on the radio playing the fiddle and from that time on, he pressed his father to buy him a fiddle. At first, Ameen's father resisted the young teenager's request simply because there was a shortage of money in their household. His father, however, said to Ameen that we will save enough money so that in time, the youngster will have that fiddle in his hands and when that time comes, Ameen can play the fiddle to his heart's content. Ameen did, eventually, get his fiddle and each day, for several hours, he would practise on that fiddle.

Ameen Ganam's practising made him an exceptional fiddler and as the years moved on, "King" Ganam would be playing with other musicians at numerous weddings as well as many barn dances. He became better and better every time, he played that fiddle and, eventually, he would get an unexpected break where he was hired to play on a country music radio show and from that show he would move on to playing the fiddle on a television show. Both Dad and myself believed that he became the main fiddle player on the TV show called "Holiday Ranch". Several years later, Ameen "King" Ganam thrilled television audiences when he got his own television show called, "Country Hoedown", where he was one of the show's main performers. When each of these shows started, Ameen would be playing his fiddle and, at that point of the show, the camera would zoom in on Ameen's face and this is when the "King" would wink in the camera sending some type of greeting to his audience. Years later, his sister Dr. Lila Fahlman would write a book about his life called, "The Fiddler with a Wink".

In the words of Joe Shoctor, the founder of Edmonton's Citadel Theatre, he said that Ameen "King" Ganam got his title "King" by winning a World Fiddle Competition in Vancouver, B.C. in the early 1950's. Ameen "King" Ganam showed so much talent as a songwriter, composer and musician for several decades and he was, in time, nominated to Canada's Country Music Hall of Honour.

On this particular day as well, Dad remembered the name, Jim Darwish. Jim, according to Pop was another of those early Lebanese pioneers. Dad referred to him as a furtrader who lived a number of years in Canada's Northwest Territories. Dad, also, said that Jim Darwish operated some type of trading post while he lived in the North. I didn't learn much more about Jim on this day other than he is buried in Edmonton's first Muslim cemetery called the Beechmount Cemetery. This cemetery is probably, as well, the first Muslim cemetery to be developed in all of Canada. Jim Darwish, a Muslim pioneer of Canada's north, was born in 1885 in Lebanon and died in Canada in 1944.

Continuing on with our stories, Mom and Dad had a number of non-Lebanese friends who came and visited us at our home. I, vaguely, remember a quite jovial fellow who came to visit one day whose name was Louis. When he came to the house, he always liked to talk and tell stories. I recall one of his stories that went like this. Louis started his story by saying that at one time, he was returning to Canada from the United States. The official, at the point of entry, into Canada asked Louis if he had anything to declare. This gentlemen declared everything except for one item and that one item was a bottle of liquor which I assume you had to pay a custom duty on. Louis while, jokingly, telling this story said that he didn't have any money to pay for the custom duty. So what did Louis do at that point in time? He, hurriedly, took his bottle of liquor back to the American side of the border and began to drink the liquor there. After several hours on the American side, where he finished his bottle of liquor, he walked back to the Canadian side without any sign of the bottle he, originally, had and in no time at all he was back home in Canada. Louis, according to Dad, ended his story by saying that Louis had some difficulty in walking a straight line when he crossed the border.

Albert Nasserdean (this is the correct spelling of his last name) was another interesting character with a Lebanese background. On numerous occasions, Albert would come and visit my parents, and he would always come in a truck which was loaded with a big supply of fruits and vegetables. Before he came to our house, however, he travelled down a few blocks of the back alleys, and then he would get out of his truck and walk to the backdoor of each house along the way and asked the housekeeper if he or she would like to buy some of his produce. If the houseowner wanted to purchase the fruits and vegetables, that person would walk to the truck, and, once there, Albert would show them the produce he had for sale.

Albert, the Lebanese salesman, repeated this process for each home he went to. Dad felt that Albert Nasserdean made a lot of money from the selling of his produce. There is no doubt, in my mind, that Albert was one of the first salespersons to sell fruits and vegetables going door to door, in a number of Edmonton neighborhoods.

As Dad continued on with his stories, he reminded me that there was, also, an Italian family, related to Louis, known as the Camillo family which came to our house for visits. Mr. and Mrs. Camillo had some very talented children who could play musical instruments such as the accordian and violin and, as well a number of their family members were very good singers. Whenever they came to visit, the children of their family would spend a lot of time entertaining us by playing enjoyable music and singing great songs. In time, the Camillo family would move to Vancouver, B.C., and I can't really say if my parents and the Camillo family maintained contact in the months and years that would lie ahead.

After listening to these stories, Dad and I made our way home. When we got home that day, Mom was resting, so Dad and I went into the living room where Dad made some comments about Mom and himself. His comments took him back to the days when he had his stores. He didn't hesitate in saying that he spent a lot of hours at the stores. Mom, on the other hand, would look after more new family members who were born during the early years of their married life. Dad told me that our family in those early days led a pretty good life with a certain amount of success until the 1930's came into, not only their lives, but, also the lives of a huge number of other individuals. These people, including my family, would now begin living their lives in the period of history that would become known as the Great Depression or as some people called it, the dirty thirties. At this point, both Dad and myself were quite tired out. We, then, made our way upstairs for what I thought was a well-deserved rest. Mom, also, continued on with her rest.

The Day That Followed

The next day, Dad and I moved ahead with what now seemed to be a routine daily walk along a path when and where stories continued to be told. As we walked at the start of that day, I thought that Dad was going to tell me more about life in the Great Depression period. For some unknown reason, however, Dad really didn't tell me that much about what took place in their lives during that time. Perhaps, he remained more on the silent side because by 1939 we had thirteen children in the family and probably this number of children kept Mom and Dad occupied with most, if not all of the free time they may have had. Dad, however, did stress upon me during his storytelling periods that he spent a lot of time in the store trying to make ends meet. It was on this day, that Dad repeated several times in a very strong voice, that things at that time did not always go as well as possible on many of those days. Dad, also, didn't hesitate in saying that those days were often very dark days. He said that many people at this time just didn't have enough money to buy things even if they might have needed them. As he continued to tell his stories on this day, he kept repeating out loud, "Yes, my son, those days were really the dark days in my life!" As Dad said these words, I felt that his words were loaded with some frustration and at the same time he seemed to express a certain amount of sadness.

No matter how disappointed Dad may have been that day, he couldn't resist talking about what he termed a miracle. This miracle would bring the Edmonton Muslim community together in order to have important discussions about how they wanted to save their culture and religion in their new homeland of Canada. Dad then provided me with some important background information.

He said in the years 1937 and 1938, a number of Muslims, including himself, had already made Edmonton their permanent home. Some of these Muslims were the peddlers, as well as the storekeepers, but there was, also, another group of Muslims who decided to go into the fur trade business. This group of Muslims made contact with the indigenous population and started to acquire the skills from the natives which were needed to trap the furbearing animals. Some of the furtrading Muslims, also, took time to learn the spoken language of the natives. These Muslims believed that business matters could be developed a lot easier when you knew the language of the people you were dealing with.

The Muslim furtraders, in time, started to travel north out of Edmonton and went into areas like Lac La Biche, Conklin and Fort McMurray in order to work on their furtrading skills. Many of these Muslim furtraders were very successful and, then, they eventually, returned to Edmonton in order to be with their fellow Muslim friends. They continued for a number of years, to travel back and forth from Edmonton to the lands of the north and during that time period, they developed themselves into excellent furtraders with expert skills.

Some Muslims, as time went on, decided to make their homes in Lac La Biche and started to open up mink ranches, which were very successful for numerous years.

Whenever the Muslims gathered in Edmonton, they started to have a number of conversations about their Arab culture and their religion of Islam. They, no doubt, had great love for their adopted home of Canada, but at the same time, they felt that their Arab culture and their religion of Islam could possibly disappear from their new way of life.

The conversations of culture and religion continued on for a number of months and soon some of the Muslims were saying that they should either build a community centre while others said that they should build a mosque. After much debate the group decided that the community should build the mosque. The mosque, which was the first to be built in Canada, would become known as the Al Rashid and would be built in such a way where the main floor would be made for religious purposes and the basement would serve the non-religious activities, such as wedding receptions. Thus, the newly-constructed mosque, which officially opened in December of 1938, would now help preserve their Arab culture as well as their Islamic religion.

The Al Rashid Mosque would take approximately ten weeks to be built at a total cost of $6,550. This price of

$6,550 included the cost of the land the mosque sat on. The Muslims would pay $550 to the City of Edmonton for two pieces of property that the mosque would be built on, located at 102 Street and 108 Avenue. The construction costs for the Al Rashid Mosque would amount to $4,800 and the community would then spend $1,200 on supplies such as rugs, tables, chairs and a furnace which would be placed in the basement of the building.

The Al Rashid, in time, would now lead the way for many more new mosques to be added to our Canadian landscape and, in addition, it would be the inspiration behind the growth of the many new Muslim communities which would develop all across Canada. Although there is no historical doubt that the Al Rashid was Canada's first mosque to be built, we Canadians can not claim to have built the first mosque in North America. Two of the first mosques to be built in North America were the mosques built in Ross, North Dakota in 1929 and the Mother Mosque of America built in Cedar Rapids, Iowa in 1934.

After telling me this information about Canada's first mosque, Dad then moved onto a story about one of his close friends. This is how Dad told me his friend's story.

One of the Muslim pioneers who was a furtrader and who came to Edmonton every so often to visit his fellow Muslims was a Lebanese immigrant by the name of Bedouin Ferran. Bedouin, however, would be given the Christian name of Peter Baker as his life started to evolve in the Canadian areas where he lived.

Peter Baker, eventually, settled in Yellowknife, Northwest Territories and in 1964 he was elected to the Territorial Council at the age of seventy-six. During his time, as an elected Councillor, Peter pushed the idea that Yellowknife should be made the capital city of the Northwest Territories. In addition, he was the first person to supply oranges to the northern natives. As well, this Muslim was responsible for providing the delivery of mail to the various communities of the north over a several year period. In time, this mail delivery on Peter's part would cause him to become snowblind. Suffering from being snowblind, Peter decided to go to Rochester, New York for an operation on his eyes. While awaiting for his eye surgery, his heart gave out and, unfortunately, he passed away at that time. When Peter Baker died in 1973 at the age of eighty-five, the Al Rashid Mosque in Edmonton had a special memorial service for him. He is buried in Yellowknife and history will always refer to him by his nickname, "The Arctic Arab".

My Dad and Peter Baker, the Arctic Arab, always had a friendly relationship that covered many years. Whenever Peter came to Edmonton, he would spend a lot of time at our house recalling stories about his life in Canada. Dad always told me that he loved to listen to Peter's stories because they were so interesting and at different times, they, also were packed with amusing adventures.

Stories About the Family Members

That day the stories continued to be told to me by my father as we walked along that well-travelled path which I now nicknamed the "Path of the Storytellers". Dad, suddenly, said to me as we walked, "You know, son, a number of people showed some puzzlement as to why Mom and he had a family with so many children!" Through Dad's eyes, however, he had great praise for a large family because he believed that a large family would be able to accomplish many interesting things over time. He was of the firm belief that the children had a significant importance in providing resources for the family as a whole. Alex, the oldest member of the family who was in his early twenties, could, for example, find a pretty good job and this job would add to the family's income. The younger members of the family could provide some help in the limited jobs they were assigned at home while the other older members, like Mickey, Minnie and Emily could work at certain jobs which would allow them to earn a small amount of money. Most of the money, that the children made, seemed to have gone into the supporting of the household, itself, and helping out the younger family members. Dad always insisted, however, that these working family members would be able to keep a suitable amount of their earnings so that they could buy things of their choices, even though the choices may have been limited.

We had thirteen family members living at home at this time. The girls in the family included my sisters, Minnie, Emily, Mona, Lily and

Zina. The boys in the family were Alex, Mickey, Jimmy, the fraternal twins, Eddie and Teddy, Sine, Kemal and myself, Richard. I was born in November of 1939. With my birth, I became the thirteenth living member of our family. I don't know if being number thirteen on the family ladder was a lucky or unlucky situation for me, but when I look back over my life, I consider myself to be one lucky human being where I was able to have, during my lifetime, a very loving Mom and Dad, as well as, brothers and sisters, who, generally, cared for each other. Sure, we had our arguments at times, but no argument was so serious that we didn't stop interacting with each other during the years that stretched into the future. I, personally, find it rather sad when I read about or hear stories of family members who don't talk to each other for years. Thank, God, our family never faced this type of experience.

The fourteenth child, who is my sister, Lila, was born in 1942. Her birth would make her the youngest member of our family.

When it came to educating our family members, Mom and Dad often told us that they had no opportunity to be educated in any kind of a formal education system, either private or public.

Both Mom and Dad, however, insisted that all family members must receive some education in a formal setting. Dad, following his religious Islamic roots, knew the value of education when he said that the Prophet Muhammad believed that a person should be educated from cradle to grave. So each of the family's children started to receive their education within the Public School System. The education for some of the children would be made up of the regular academic subjects such as Math, Science and Geography. Alex and Mickey would be trained more in the area of business. As these two brothers got older, in age, Dad told me that he got both brothers a job with a Jewish business person called Hymie Weisler. As the years moved on, Mr. Weisler would go out of business and Mickey and Alex then took over the location where Weisler's business was located.

Hymie Weisler was a businessman that Dad had known while spending time in Winnipeg and Brandon. My father always had a good business relationship with Weisler in Manitoba and they maintained a very cordial and friendly relationship over the years. That relationship continued to exist even after both families, eventually, set up new homes in Edmonton. Dad, as stated earlier, opened his first store in Edmonton and then there was a second store that he opened and after that store, Dad would open several more stores as the years passed by. How many stores he opened, and closed, I am unable to say. In his conversations with me, Pop indicated simply that he had opened and operated several stores over a number of years. Hymie Weisler, on the other hand, opened a very big supply store where he sold to many more customers on a monthly basis than my Dad would sell to his customers probably over a six-month time period. No matter what, the relationship between Dad and Weisler, allowed Alex and Mickey to get involved with an excellent understanding of the business world, which, as the years rolled on, allowed my two oldest brothers to open several businesses in both Edmonton and Calgary. In addition, to getting involved in the business world, both of these brothers would make their way onto the social scene of Edmonton, as well as the political arena, where they would support candidates running for political office, but they always insisted that they were never interested in running for political office themselves.

Both of these brothers, did, indeed, become members of numerous organizations. Within each organization they joined, these two brothers were the ones who contributed numerous ideas to the running of each organization they participated in. Both brothers were well accepted by the many organizations they became involved with. Mickey would shine a bit more in the public eye than Alex did and for several years, he was in charge of organizing the Edmonton Exhibition Parade each July when he served as a member of the local organization known as Edmonton Northlands. Mickey, also, was very good at public speaking while Alex shied away from this type of activity.

Mickey and Alex would both work with Mr. Weisler for a number of years—how many years, I can't really be specific in saying. Dad, however, when asked the question about the length of time, those two sons worked for Weisler, would supply an answer that simply came out as, they worked with this man for many years. As the years kept rolling along, a third brother, Eddie, would work for Weisler alongside his two older brothers. For every year that these three brothers worked with Weisler, each of them would acquire more and more business skills. After this story, Dad and I headed for home.

My Brothers Get to Own a Business or Two

On another day, when Dad and I again journeyed on one of our storytelling walks, he, suddenly, said to me out of the blue, "Young fellow, you know my friend Hymie Weisler grew older just as we all do, and he felt that he just wasn't interested where he wanted to continue running his business." Weisler then left his business and it wouldn't be long before Mickey and Alex started to run their own business out of where Weisler's business was located. I am uncertain as to where or how my brother, Eddie, fitted into this new situation. The question I am seeking an answer for is did Eddie become a partner in this new business or did he continue to work as an employee? No matter what, we can now say that this new venture was open for business.

The two older brothers thus started their new business venture by packaging smaller toys into individual plastic bags and began to refer to these packaged toys as super-value toys. It should be noted that before starting their new business venture at the Weisler location, Mickey and Alex had some type of small business located in the area of 101 Street and between 107th Avenue and 108th Avenue. At this location, I remember that my mother use to cook food for their small staff and on my way back to Victoria Composite High School for my afternoon classes, I would carry a large plate of food to the business for the staff to eat. I, vaguely, remember eating some of that food as I carried it to the location where the business was. It was at this business location that Evelyn, Mickey's wife, and June, Alex's wife, worked at packaging many kinds of items.

Returning to the super-value toys, these toys would be sold to numerous stores and were placed on wire racks using metal prongs to keep the items in place. The racks, themselves, could be placed on a stand of some sort and were approximately three feet in height and up to two and a half feet wide. There would be a number of prongs coming out of each rack. Each packaged toy would have a label covering the top of the bag and there would be a hole in the middle of the label. Each labelled packaged toy could now be slid onto a prong and each prong could hold up to as many as a dozen packaged toys, depending on their size. On one rack alone well over one hundred toys could be found, very nicely displayed. The pricing of the toys would vary from twenty-five cents to a couple of dollars. To ensure that this part of their new idea would be successful, they hired several salesmen who would try to sell to as many stores as possible a wire rack full of toys. They were, also, aware that in order for this part of the business to be successful, they would have to service the toy supply on a regular basis in order to make certain that each rack was always full of toys. Mickey and Alex were, undoubtedly, of the firm belief that if a business was to be successful, you had to offer the storekeepers the best possible service available. Furthermore, it was, also, their belief that the better your service was, the more your business would grow. The super-value toy racks proved to be extremely successful and would continue to be successful for a number of years into the future. In time, however, their success would be challenged by competitors who picked up on the brother's ideas as time slipped away.

Mickey and Alex, at this point, decided to add new inventories to their super-value toy racks by starting to purchase huge amounts of toys from manufacturers located in eastern Canada. Dad was told by Mickey that most of those toys they brought in from the eastern part of Canada seemed to have been manufactured in the provinces of Ontario and Quebec. Some of the toys did, however, come from the United States. In addition to the toys, the young owners still in the old Weisler location, would purchase quantities of dry goods, such as shirts and pants, which now became part of the regular inventory. These drygood items were, also, made in Canada. It is of importance to know that several of the dry good manufacturers were of Arab origin and this fact made it a lot easier for my brothers to purchase from these suppliers, because our family, itself, has an Arab-Ukrainian origin. Also, it seems as if there is some type of a kinship relation when it comes to Arabs working with each other in the world of business. Knowing these Arab manufacturers allowed Mickey and Alex to make new contacts for suppliers easier because it seems that if you knew one manufacturer in those early days, it was easy to get to know many other manufacturers. Knowing all of these manufacturers made it easier on the company the brothers operated for them to get acceptable credit rating terms and, also, they would be able to purchase more manufactured bargains whenever they became available.

Mickey and Alex continued to add new items, such as hardware ones, to the supplies they would now sell. The variety of goods they now sold started to become much larger in numbers and soon they would turn their new business into a company called Western Varieties and Dry Goods Wholesale Ltd. A line of jewellery, also, would be added to the items now being sold at their business.

With the start of this newly-named company, Mickey and Alex would begin to hire family members to help run the business. Eddie, it seems, was the first to be added seeing as how he had business experience working for Weisler. A short time later, the brothers decided to open a related business in Calgary. Eddie would then be asked to run the Calgary operation of the family business. After Eddie, Jimmy joined the company. He would travel with his suitcases, loaded with samples in each case and make his way by car and/or station wagon to various parts of Northern Alberta, in addition to various regions of British Columbia along with travelling to Whitehorse in the Yukon Territory as well as Yellowknife in the Northwest Territories. When this section of Western Varieties started to build up, Mickey and Alex then hired several more salesmen to help Jimmy cover the massive territory he was looking after on his own. In addition, some of the salesmen, also, would take their turn at filling up the wire racks with the super-value toys.

After bringing Jimmy into the business, the two owners brought their brother, Ted, into the expanding business. Ted, previously, had worked for a business called Dower Brothers which was located right across the street from Western Varieties. When asked to become part of the new family business, Ted did not hesitate in joining this growing venture. Ken, known as Kemal, in the Arabic language would be next to join the business and before he joined, this younger brother was employed as an insurance salesman for Equitable Life and he had learned a lot of his insurance knowledge from a great Edmonton Eskimos football legend called Frank Anderson. My sister, Lila, would be the last of the family members to join Western Varieties after she completed her high school education.

In the future years, Lila became a very valuable member of the family team when she would start to spend weeks in Calgary where Eddie had now opened up a branch of the family's business venture. Eddie required some much needed assistance because of the growing success of the business in that city. This newly-formed business in Calgary, although part of Western Varieties, would now go under another name.

After Western Varieties was established and started to grow, Mickey and Alex looked at numerous ways of building up their business interests. They would soon open a company which they called East-West Imports. This was a company where they wanted to bring imported goods, in quantity, to numerous stores throughout several of the western provinces. The concept of this company was an excellent one, but the brothers found difficulties in making it work to their advantage. The East-West Import Company was, eventually, shut down and Mickey and Alex looked at a completely different idea that would complement the Western Varieties Wholesale business. Their new idea would lead to a new business opening up in the basement of the same building as where Western Varieties was located. This new business would be called Alberta Giftwares Ltd. (Edmonton) and its name for advertising purposes would show the name Alberta Giftwares Ltd. along with a picture of a genie holding a pillow which could carry a gift item. After opening Alberta Giftwares in Edmonton, Eddie, in time, would open a branch of this business in Calgary.

Stories About Pop

As Dad and I sat on that bench in the park, on what was a sunny Tuesday afternoon, where we recalled more of our family history, Dad pushed his elbow into my left side and said to me, "Come on, my son, let's go for a walk so we can tell more stories as we walk in the direction of home." As we walked together along that particular path, Dad started to tell me more about his own life. I should emphasize that even though I had heard some of his story before, Pop was now ready to add more of the missing parts to that story. My Dad started talking by reminding me that his life started in Canada when he set foot in his new homeland back in 1901. He, vividly, remembered that he was just a young nineteen year old teenager in that year. Dad, also, said that he was an Arab immigrant looking for a new type of life which he hoped would be different than the type of life he had led in Lebanon. Dad, further repeated, that Lebanon at that time, was part of the greater Syrian Empire, which itself was found within the larger Turkish Ottoman Empire. Pop now starts to tell me about those first days when he arrived in Canada. As we move along in our stories, Dad will continue to give more details of his early Canadian life and he will, at times, be the person who tells the story, but at other times, I will step in to continue with the telling of his story. I, his youngest son, will attempt to move each of his stories along where I can express what his words might have been as if he, personally, was still telling the story himself. The word, I, from now on will be used often at times in the rest of our stories and needless to say, this word will always refer to me telling the story whenever the word is used.

It is my belief that Dad always thought of himself, from the time he first arrived in Canada, as a very proud person who strongly believed in the religion of Islam and he made certain that he always followed his religion to the best of his ability for the rest of his life. There is, also, no doubt in my mind, that Dad had memorized the whole Qur'an, which is the Holy book for the Muslims. I can, vividly, recall Dad sitting in his chair at home, on numerous occasions, with his two hands opened and held close together, and in a very strong voice, he recited parts of the Holy Book. While the recitation was going on, my Dad's voice sounded throughout the room. I listened, carefully, as my father continued on with his recitations and when he is finished, he says to me, "My son, please make me a cup of coffee!". In order to fulfill his request, I moved quickly into the kitchen and made that requested cup of coffee for him. In addition, to his cup of coffee, I offered him a tasty snack which he took without any hesitation. In the years of the past, my Mother would do these tasks for Dad but when she past away in 1964, this responsibility fell on the shoulders of my sister, Lila, as well as myself. The two of us together would now accept the responsibility of caring for our Dad.

When Lila and I were both home at the same time, the two of us would share in doing things that Dad might have wanted done. Quite often, Dad would move from his living room chair into the kitchen. There, in the kitchen, Pop would sit in the chair he always occupied and then maybe he would ask for a cup of coffee and more often than not, with Lila and myself sitting around the table with him, our beloved father would start to recall numerous events that took place in his life and, at times, he would surprise us by even telling stories about Lila and myself. He, always, had stories galore to tell and these stories usually centred around our family members, friends of the family and a lot of the Arab pioneers whom Dad had known over the years.

Stories About My Sisters

Our family was a huge family, and as, previously mentioned there were six daughters and eight sons. By the time the younger members of the family, such as Lila and myself, started growing older in age, some of the already older children were, of course, growing older at the same time and soon the time came when several of them were leaving home in order to pursue a new type of life. My sister, Minnie, known, also, by her Arabic name of Fatima, would marry at quite a young age to an older fellow by the name of Charlie Joseph. Dad and Mom, from my understanding of this situation, were not in favour of the marriage, but it took place anyway. Our parents felt that Minnie was just too young to get married at the time.

The newlyweds lived in Edmonton, but very seldom were there ever any family visits taking place. Charlie would open a grocery store and he and Minnie worked hard to make it a success. My niece, Donna was one of the children born from the marriage of Minnie and Charlie, and she turned out to be a very creative person, who, always, treated me with the utmost respect and love. It was a very sad occasion for me when Donna passed away. With her passing, I lost a dear niece and an extremely close friend. I, also, had a very good relationship with another of Minnie's daughters. Her name was Irma. With her passing I lost another close family member.

My sisters, Lily and Zina both would marry Americans and after their marriages took place, they moved to the United States where both couples ended up in the same city called Fort Wayne, Indiana. Every so often both of these couples would return to Edmonton for a family visit. Zina's husband, Byron, even tried for a while to make Edmonton their permanent home. When things didn't work out for them in Edmonton, they decided to move back to Fort Wayne. Lily and Joe came to visit us on several different occasions and I, always, found it to be a great pleasure to have them stay with us in the family home while they were on their visits here. By the way, Lily's Arabic name was Mariam. Joe, her husband, was employed as a fireman and one of his favourite activities was fishing.

My sister, Emily, never got married even though she seemed to have been involved in several romances. It is my belief that Emily never got married because she was too dedicated to her work. She left Edmonton at a younger age in order to go and live in Washington, D.C., with her friend Audrey Petit. The two of them became employees of the World Bank whose offices were in Washington. Emily's employment would give her the opportunity to travel to numerous places throughout the world. On missions sponsored by the World Bank, Emily would do work in Ethiopia, Kenya, Uganda and the Philippines. Emily was, without a doubt, in my opinion, one of the most caring people that I have ever known throughout my entire lifetime. Whenever she travelled to various places, she would always send me information from these places and she would, as well, write me all kinds of letters from these locations. Her job, at the World Bank, specifically, was to be part of a mission to each country some of the employees travelled to and the mission, itself, had the responsibility of providing financial assistance to the developing countries, at that time, so that each country had a chance to build itself up as it worked on its development.

Because of Emily's interest in getting information to me, I developed, over the years, a great knowledge about foreign places. Emily made it possible for me to learn a lot about Ethiopia, Kenya, Uganda, Tanzania (known as Tanganika at the time), the Philippines and numerous other places. My sister, Emily, also was a great photographer and she loved to have a slide show presentation for the family whenever she returned to Edmonton.

Earlier on, I provided some information about my sister, Minnie, more in connection with her married life. At this time, I would now like to provide information about my sister, Minnie, more as the individual who she was. Minnie was my oldest sister and she tended to be a very strong—willed individual. She was a kind person, but she always felt that most of the things she said were generally, always right. My sister operated several grocery stores throughout her lifetime and she had the opportunity to deal with all kinds of people while operating the stores. Her last store was in a location not too far from where I went to Junior High School. At times, I used, to walk from the school to her store where she offered me some food and/or a bottle of Coca Cola. She, herself, had a loving affection for Coca Cola, which at the time, only came in a glass bottle. I still have one of those Coca Cola bottles from her store because I saved it from years ago. The reason why I saved this particular bottle is because the bottle cap was not put straight on top of the bottle. Half of the cap was put on properly but the other half was flattened out. This bottle had some Coca Cola in it and even today, some of that Coca Cola still exists in this bottle, although the rest of the pop disappeared from the bottle over the years.

Minnie spent most of her life in Edmonton and only did a limited amount of travelling. She was an excellent cook, and I, as well as other family members, always loved the fancy pastry she made. Her pastry, without a doubt, was constantly loaded with the strength of being extremely delicious.

With Minnie's story coming to an end, Dad, Lila and myself took a look at the clock and noticed that it was a little past our bedtime. We then said to each other, "It's time to go to bed. We will continue on with our stories at another time!" So off to bed the three of us went that night.

<u>Stories About Lila and Me</u>

When I was in my room, I couldn't fall asleep. I started to think about other family stories. Somewhere along the way, I started to concentrate on a story about Lila and myself. As noted earlier, my sister, Lila, was the youngest of the girls in our family, and she was, also, the youngest member of the whole family.

When Lila and I were in our early years of life, ages eight and ten years, I remember that we would get some money from Dad. It wasn't hard for me to ask Dad for that money in order for Lila and me to go to the movies. He, usually, was in bed, semi-asleep, when I requested the money. He never, ever, hesitated to give me that money at anytime. The money he wanted to give me was always in the form of coins which were kept in his right front pocket of his pants. The pants were, usually, hanging on a long metal nail, two or three feet above the level of his head. I would get a chair, stand on it and then reached into his pocket of coins. Feeling all of those coins in the pant pocket, made me feel like a small-time crook, because I took more coins than I should have out of that pocket from Dad's pants. Unfortunately, this would be my first act of what I consider to be stealing. Thank God, this act of stealing never turned me into a professional thief as I grew older.

With that money, Lila and I would travel several blocks from our home, on a Saturday afternoon, and then we would climb a long load of stairs which were placed in a steep hill that separated our home from where several movie theatres were located. After climbing the stairs, we would have another one or two blocks to go before we reached one of the theatres found along Jasper Avenue. There were probably four theatres in this area at that time. I remember the names of these movie houses quite well since we went to these theatres quite often. There was the Empress, the Capitol, the Rialto and my favourite movie theatre of all, the Strand.

For me, the Strand was the best theatre because every Saturday afternoon, it would have a double-feature where one of the movies was always a cowboy movie. The second movie was either another cowboy movie or a comedy featuring actors like the Marx Brothers. Separating the two movies would be a cartoon starring characters such as Mighty Mouse, Bugs Bunny, Donald Duck, Goofy, Porky Pig, Woody Woodpecker and, the cat and mouse team called Tom and Jerry. Felix, the cat, was, also, included in this group. The cowboy movies which Lila and I saw had stars such as Gene Autry, Roy Rogers, Lash Larue, Sunset Carson, Red Ryder and my favourite cowboy of all, the Durango Kid. Also, starring in the movies was another favourite of mine, none other than Randolph Scott.

With my sister, Lila and I watched those movies over the many weeks, months and years that we journeyed up those stairs leading to the theatres, and we would always say to each other that for every movie we would watch, we always wanted the "good guys" to defeat the "bad guys". I really enjoyed those good old movie days and I think I can say without any hesitation at all, that Lila loved those movies as well. Those really were the good old days when fifteen cents would get us into the theatres and five cents would give us the opportunity to purchase a bag of popcorn or a chocolate bar. Thanks to Dad, we always had enough money to get us into the theatres, and, also, thanks to our Mother who never stopped us from going to those movies and who made it possible for us to always enjoy life outside of our homesetting.

When Lila and I aged by several years, we stopped going to the movies on those Saturday afternoons. One of the reasons why we stopped is that we had moved from the house that was within walking distance from the theatres. If we now had any interest in going to the movies together, we would have to travel by bus to get us to our destination. At this point in time in our lives, the Saturday afternoon movies, it now seems, would have to be an item shoved into our past lives.

With the movie days out of our lives, Lila and I continued on with our educational careers. My sister, would, in time, complete Grade 12 and, thus, be able to graduate from high school. I too, would complete Grade 12 and then I would go to university. It was my desire at the time, to be a doctor, but, unfortunately, I just didn't seem to have enough ability to achieve my doctor's goal.

At the University of Alberta, in Edmonton, I registered in the Faculty of Arts and majored in Sociology which gave me the opportunity to learn a lot about human behavior. I even learned a great deal about myself by taking numerous courses in both the Sociology and Psychology areas.

University life wasn't the easiest life for me and I would be lying if I didn't tell people that I had to struggle, in order to achieve, throughout my university years. I was, however, determined to succeed at university and, succeed, I did. I ended up getting a Bachelor of Arts degree where I majored in Sociology. With this degree I then went out into the working world trying to get a job. Unfortunately, I was unable to get any employment that was suitable for me. I got my Sociology degree in 1964.

Since I was unable to get any suitable employment, I decided to return to university and this time I registered in the Faculty of Education. I really do not know, exactly, why I entered the educational faculty other than, that I thought, it would lead me to a job. As well, there, also, seemed to have been a shortage of teachers at this particular time, especially in the elementary level. At university, I registered in the elementary area and from that time forward, I worked very hard at getting my degree in education. In the spring of 1966, I earned my Education Degree. That degree made it possible for me to get employment with the Edmonton Public School Board. I got my first teaching job in a school where I started teaching my very first class in September of 1966. It was a grade five class at a school called Laurier Heights. The school, itself, was an Elementary-Junior High School.

My class, that year in 1966, was a mix of very high achievers as well as some students who required extra help with their learning. My first principal was a Mr. Bill Coull. A very interesting point about Bill Coull is that he taught me Grade Five at Donald Ross School in the Rossdale community where I grew up. It is my belief that I went on to become a pretty good teacher, in that first teaching year as well as the next several years because of the help given to me by the numerous students I taught along with their parents and the great teaching staff that I worked with. At times, over the years, I have met former students who told me that I made a positive influence in their own lives.

Other Family Stories

I was only one of two members from my family who went to university and graduated from the learning institution. My brother, Ken (Kemal), tried to become a dentist when he enrolled at the University of Alberta, but after one year he gave this desire up and did not pursue any further studies at a university.

The only other member of the family who went on to university and to graduate from the learning centre was my brother, Sine. He, too, graduated as a teacher and most of his teaching was done in the Junior High area. In his early years of teaching, he went off to the country of Ghana and taught school there. He then returned to Edmonton and taught for a number of years with the Edmonton Public School Board. Sine, also, taught with the Edmonton Separate School Board and at one point, in his teaching career, he moved to Calgary, Alberta and spent several years teaching in that city. A lot of Sine's teaching years were spent teaching Special Education students.

At Sine's retirement function in 1994, a dedication book was published by the School Board and in that book, it gave the following information about Sine.

"As a teacher at Stratford, Westminster, Highlands, Parkview and Youngstown schools, Sine became known for his positive attitude and keen sense of humour. As a co-operative team member, he was always willing to support and assist with the total school program. He was, also, appreciated for his strong support of the district and his devotion to special education students.

During Sine's twenty-nine year teaching career, he was committed and dedicated to the profession."

My sister, Mona, got married to a person of Icelandic descent by the name of Barney Loftson. I, personally, found Barney to be a pretty good guy and got along with him quite well over the years. Mona and Barney moved from Edmonton to Winnipeg during the early years of their marriage. After moving to Winnipeg, the couple would return on several occasions to Edmonton for a visit with the rest of the family.

Early in Mona's life, some type of accident came about which affected Mona's eyesight. She never ended up totally blind, but she was considered to have lost enough of her eyesight and the Canadian National Institute for the Blind (CNIB) considered her to be legally blind. Before Mona married, she had a very large group of friends, who were, also, blind. In addition, many of these friends had their own friends and several marriages took place within these friendly groups over the years. There were friends like Esther Clark, who worked for the provincial government and she married Alex Gemmell who was both blind as well as hard of hearing. Another friend, by the name of Helen, married Walter Sorenson, who had a seeing eye-dog which helped Walter move along the streets of Edmonton.

There were many other friends and, I, always remember one of the most exciting things about them as a group. Several of them were able to play numerous musical instruments. Mona, when she was still single, sometimes would invite them to the house and they would have snacks and then they would start playing their musical instruments. The sound of their beautiful music would then flow into the evening air, and I would with all sincerity, like to add, that the music was so lively that, as you listened to it, you could imagine in your mind all kinds of people dancing and/or singing to the sounds of the music.

Dad and Mom never objected to Mona's friends coming to the house on those numerous occasions. The music gatherings lived on for quite a while and would only come to an end when some of the musically-talented individuals passed away.

When it comes to Mona, I never was told by anybody in the family how Mona lost some of her eyesight. After she married and returned to Edmonton for visits with her children, Mona and I became much closer even though there was some difference in our ages. When I think about it, I believe my relationships with the sisters, who came to Edmonton for their visits, were quite strong simply because I was home a lot and I had the time to spend with them where I could talk to them on a one to one basis or drive them downtown or to a meeting with a friend of theirs.

When I think back to those times, I never thought about how lucky I was to have these many experiences where I was often surrounded by so many people who were part of my own family as well as those non-family members who were always close in friendship to us. It has to be emphasized that many of these family friends remained as friends for a lifetime and even those surviving friends today, whenever I see them, they like to talk about the good old days. They continue to want to know about the ones who are still living today.

<u>The Days That Followed</u>

The next few days were cloudy ones where the sun occasionally broke through the heavy mass of clouds. Dad and I were still in the house, drinking our coffee, when Dad suggested that we go for a walk so that more stories could be told. I agreed with Dad and once outside we walked along a narrow path for a good length of time. We asked each other a number of questions and, suddenly, Dad stopped walking. I asked him if he was okay. He replied, "Yes! I am doing great." He then reached into one of his pockets and pulled out one of the many pipes that he owned. He loved to smoke his pipes on a regular basis and when you looked at his pipes, you could see the wear and tear these pipes seemed to have endured throughout their lifetime.

Standing beside me, with his pipe in hand, he took a package of tobacco from his suitcoat pocket and then loaded some of that tobacco into the bowl of the pipe. Dad seemed to always love filling his pipe and lighting it in order to have a number of good puffs of smoke. As Dad continued to stand there, with pipe in hand, I watched him move his eyes around and I began to wonder what he was thinking. It wasn't really that long before I realized that he was searching for a place to sit. You see we had been walking for a certain length of time on this particular day and Dad, also, seemed to be a bit tired out. He then grabbed my right arm and started to pull me in the direction of a bench, which was partially hidden behind some branches of a large tree that had an abundance of overhanging branches. We, eventually, made it to the bench and Dad gently lowered himself onto that bench with his pipe gripped tightly by his clutching hand. He then smiled at me and kind of chuckled to himself and said, "Sit down, my son!" and that is exactly what I did. I sat very close to Dad, mainly, because the bench was a bit short in length.

The Birthday Parties

After sitting for quite a few minutes, Dad smiled at me and said, "It's time for us to get on with our stories!" It was at this point that I suddenly said to Pop, "Do you remember all of those birthday parties Lila and I put on for you over the years?" His birthday was on December 22nd and Lila and I, always, insisted on having a number of people over to our house so that they could help celebrate his birthday. On those occasions, our house was always packed with numerous people and it even became quite hard at times to move around in a room of the house because each room seemed to have an endless supply of people found within them. As the years travelled on, Lila and I probably made it tougher on ourselves when we made the decision to have Mickey and Evelyn's daughter, Patty, celebrate her birthday at the same time we were celebrating Dad's birthday. I said to Dad, "Patty, one of your granddaughters, also, was born in December around the same date you were born in the month of December!"

Those birthday celebrations never ran short of food and drinks. Mickey would always make sure that he brought a good supply of sliced corn beef and salami for each party. Guests and other family members would bring pastry galore and other food dishes. Mickey's family would bring along two birthday cakes to help celebrate Dad and Patty's birthdays. I reminded Dad that there was one cake for Patty and the other cake was for him who was now being called Grampa by so many of the family members. My Dad then shouted out to me, "I, honestly, remember those days very well!" As for me, I told Pop that I remember one birthday where it snowed quite heavily. The snow amount was so great that cars would get stuck, in some cases, travelling down that road in front of the house. I, then, told Dad, on that day, I went outside and shovelled the snow off the road so that people could park their cars close to the house when they came that evening. It took me about three hours on that day to get the road cleared. Although I took some breaks during that three hour period, I never gave up the thought of getting the road ready for the visitors who were going to help celebrate Patty's and Grampa's birthdays.

After listening to what I said, Dad told me, "You know son, I really loved those days!" Right after Dad had finished these words, I spoke up and said to Pop that I loved those days as well and some of them were the best days of my life. Those really were the days when family and friends got together each year to celebrate two very happy occasions—a birthday party for my Dad, and another party for Dad's granddaughter, Patty.

In addition to the birthday parties each year, Lila and I, also, celebrated the Christmas period by inviting family members and a limited number of friends over to the house for Christmas Eve. That's the day I cooked the turkey, stuffed it with Mom's rice dressing mix recipe and when it was done, our brother, Teddy, always asked to have the crispy skin of the turkey. For some reason, Teddy just loved eating that skin, year after year. As much as I can remember, I mentioned to Dad that the Christmas period was a kind of tradition that was established by Mom and when our Mother passed away, my sister, Lila, and myself maintained this traditional time period for many years. It was a very joyous time when the family members who lived in Edmonton came to the house to celebrate special occasions and it was, also, a time when many of our relatives and friends who lived outside of Edmonton, also, came to the house to be with family members. Our sister, Emily, for example, would quite often make a journey home from her job at the World Bank in Washington, D.C. so that she could be with family and friends at these gatherings. I, then, told Dad, that Emily loved him and Mom so much that the two of them were the main reason for her visits at those times of the year. In addition, to Emily's visits, our brother, Eddie, after he moved to Calgary, would make certain that he, too, would be here on Christmas Eve in order to help celebrate our joyous time periods. At those Christmas Eve gatherings, we, always, had more than enough food available for everyone to go back for seconds and even, thirds, if they desired to do so.

One of the main characters at many of these Christmas time occasions was our cousin, Alex Amery. This is the same Alex Amery who brought those two frozen turkeys, to our house, which Mom always cooked up as the main meat dish during those great times. Mom would stuff those birds with her own great rice dressing recipe. At our gatherings, Alex, always continued to say that he could speak twenty-seven languages and kept repeating that he learned all of those languages in only one day of school. I believe that he probably could say hello or a short phrase for many of the languages, and, therefore, he was telling the truth, in a certain way, when he said he knew how to speak the twenty-seven languages. Even more amazing, Cousin Alex kept insisting that he learned all of those languages while attending school for only that one day. I loved Cousin Alex because of his great sense of humour and how, at times, he would display a fit of anger, which more often than not, was put on for a show on his part. Alex, undoubtedly, provided all of us with many laughs at those gatherings over the years.

Alex Amery, for most of his working years was self-employed. He was one of the original Arab peddlers who used Rimbey, Alberta, as a home-base when he did his peddling of the many goods he handled. During these peddling days, Alex travelled around Central Alberta with a wagon that was led by two horses. I, vaguely, remember that he called his horses, Nellie and June. Each year, my cousin Alex, would split his time between staying in Edmonton, where he, usually, stayed at Mom and Dad's in the winter time period and he would do the peddling in the warmer months of the year. In those peddling years, Alex would sell a lot of G.W.G. products, especially, cowboy shirts and jeans. Dad either arranged to sell him the G.W.G. goods or he would go to the G.W.G. factory with Alex where he had the opportunity to meet the owners of the company and then could deal with them on his own in the future. There is no doubt, in my mind, that Alex got to know a lot of people because of how genuine of a person he was. We will learn more about Cousin Alex Amery as my Dad and I continue on our journey of storytelling.

My Relationship with Dad

It was now time for our rest to come to an end as we lifted ourselves off the bench we were sitting on. Then we continued on with our walk. For the next fifteen to twenty minutes, Dad and I were kind of quiet, and for whatever reason, we didn't really say that much to each other. Perhaps, our quietness was because we took time to admire Mother Nature and all that she had to offer on our journey or maybe we were just tired out recalling all of those times related to the birthday parties as well as the parties we had during the Christmas periods.

I now began to think more about the relationship Dad and I had established with each other. I considered my Dad to be a really good guy and I now think about the times he made very enjoyable for both myself and other family members. There was over a fifty year difference in age between Dad and myself, but being the good and kind father that he was, he always treated me in a very special way.

I remember when Gene Autry, who was a very popular cowboy star came to Edmonton. Dad wanted to see Gene Autry and my father took me along with him to see this famous cowboy. On another occasion, Dad took me to the G.W.G. factory so that he could buy me a new pair of pants. I remember, very well, the following day after I got those new pants, I wore them to school where I was having a shop course of some sort. While I was doing some work for the course, there was some type of metal strip nearby and somehow I got up in such a way that the metal strip caught my new pants and made a slit, in them, about two inches long in a vertical direction and about three-quarters of an inch in the horizontal direction. Probably, at this time, I had one of those panic attack moments wondering what was going to happen to me because of the damage done to the new pants. I, honestly, don't know what happened because of the damaged pants, but I assume I would have let my Mom know the story as to how the pants got ripped and she more than likely fixed them for me. As for Dad, I never could figure out if he knew or didn't know about the ripped pants. Anyway, in the end, nothing serious came about because of the pants and life continued on its merry way for me and probably for Mom and Dad, as well.

The Shack

Another incident where Dad showed much kindness to me was when he had a storage place for his G.W.G. clothing merchandise. The storage place was located behind a barber shop on 97 Street and 102 Avenue. That storage place was nicknamed "The Shack" and Dad rented the shack space from the barber who was of Italian ancestry with the name of Florence. In that shack, which was quite small in space, was a table which took nearly one-half of the shack's floor space. Chairs were placed around the table. If my memory serves me correctly, I think there were six chairs, all of which were made out of solid wood. In addition, there was all kinds of shelving, going from floor level and going nearly as high as the ceiling. The distance from floor level to the height of the ceiling was about ten feet or in metre language about three and one-half metres. There probably were four shelves in all. Three of those shelves were loaded with clothing. These three shelves stretched over the distance of three walls and the fourth shelf did not stretch as far because there was a big doorway which allowed space for people to come and go, so in reality, that shelving had some limited room. The fourth shelving unit had lots of Dad's business records stored in numerous books. These record books, of which there were many, undoubtedly, told the stories of Dad's business years and his dealings with suppliers and customers he had known and worked with over those many years he was in business.

Getting back to the three other sections of shelving, one would notice upon examination, that the shelves were stacked with mainly G.W.G. products, especially shirts and jeans. All of the shirts, as well as the jeans, were arranged in sizes from smallest to largest. The jeans would be arranged according to waist sizes and the shirts would go from small to the extra large sizes. Dad had lots of the shirts and jeans because, they, without any doubt, were the best sellers.

In addition to the shelving there was that table and those wooden chairs Dad had in his shack. The table and chairs quite often were used for playing card games with his friends. Some of those card games, from what I heard, lasted on some occasions well into the wee hours of the morning. Dad, at times, didn't come home on those nights and I have no idea as to how Mom and my brothers and sisters reacted to this type of behavior on Dad's part.

I do, however, recall that on some Saturdays, Lila, my younger sister, and I used to go and visit Dad at the shack. Occasionally, he and his friends were playing cards when we arrived. Even though Dad seemed pleased to see Lila and me on those occasions, I am, absolutely, certain that he didn't enjoy us being in the shack while the card games were going on.

Being the smart fellow, Dad was, he kind of bribed the two of us by giving us some money which we had to spend in places away from the shack area. It wasn't really that hard to spend the money, Dad had given us.

Not that far from the shack, maybe about a block away, was a bakery called Stinson Bakery. So with our money, Lila and I would journey down the sidewalk which took us to that bakery. When we stood in front of Stinson Bakery, I, quietly, opened its door and my sister and I were, suddenly, inside this wonderful business and both of us then stared with wide-opened eyes and started to admire all of the different types of baked goods and absorbed the strong, lovely smell of all of those products as well. The one type of baked product that I will never forget was a baked piece that probably was about three inches long and two inches wide. This piece of pastry was loaded with all kinds of fruits, like cherries, and, in addition each of these pieces had all kinds of nuts in them. My sister and I really didn't have too much of a problem getting rid of the money, Dad had given us. After buying the pastry, Lila and I would head for our home eating the bought pieces of pastry along the way. Our home was, approximately, eight blocks away from where the bakery was. We continued to walk home, taking our time and we probably didn't even think about the energy we were using in order to get us home. Walking for us seemed to be a very enjoyable activity in those early days of our lives.

One of the people, who, also, went to the shack, mainly to play cards was a tall, slim person with a thin moustache known by the name of Frank Laskey. Frank was married to my cousin, Ruth Almer who hailed from Prince Albert, Saskatchewan. She was one of the daughters of Frank and Nellie Almer. Ruth and Frank would visit Edmonton several times a year. Frank was a very kind person to all of our family members and I know for sure that at times he visited the shack to play cards.

Frank Laskey was a very interesting character who showed much creativity at numerous times. I recall that he came to our house one day with a fellow having the last name of Campbell. On that day, Frank started talking to my Mom, and I listened to their conversation with some amazement. He was telling my Mom about a baked product that could have all kinds of food items put on a piece of dough. The food items included cheese, onions, tomatoes and tomato paste which was spiced up and watered-down so that it wouldn't be so thick. The thinner version of the tomato paste was spread over the dough and then the vegetables and cheese were placed on top of that water-downed tomato paste. Eventually, the dough with the food items on top of it would be placed in the oven and then baked until the dough was a real nice light brown colour. When I think of it, Frank was describing what would become known in this part of Canada as the pizza.

I want to make it clear that Frank's idea of this baked product, as far as I know, wasn't his idea to begin with, but on the other hand it could have been an idea, that he, himself, may have thought up. No matter what, it was a terrific idea and all we have to do is to think about how popular the pizza is today.

These early times, such as the days when the shack existed were really enjoyable times and showed how close of a relationship existed among friends. The shack would, eventually, close down when Florence, the barber, sold the building that housed his barbershop as well as the shack which was located in the back of that building. After the shack closed, Dad would, soon after, go into retirement. He would sell off the clothing he had in the shack and then moved his business books into the basement of a new house that Alex and Mickey had built for the family who were still living with Mom and Dad.

After the new house was completed in the Queen Mary Park area, located about two miles away from the home in Rossdale, Dad told me that he made it clear to one and all that he was now officially retired from the business world.

Retirement

Dad and I continued with our walk on that particular day and he kept telling me on several occasions, how pleased he was with the location of the new house. He said that he could walk downtown as often as he wanted to or he could take the bus to a designated destination. In addition, Canada's first mosque, the Al Rashid, wasn't that far away from our new home. As well, many of the Arab friends, such as the Hamdons, the Saddy family and Mahmoud and Mike Tarrabain were all within a short walking distance from the new house. Most of the time, however, Dad and Mom stayed at home and numerous visitors kept coming to visit them.

With so many visitors coming to the house, it wasn't really a quiet and relaxing time for either my Dad and especially, my Mom. Quite often, it seemed as if the household was invaded by those visitors. Both Mom and Dad, however, really loved having visitors over in those early years after moving into their new home. Young people, as well as the oldtimers came to visit. When the visitors arrived, they would be greeted in an extremely kind manner. Dad would soon be seated in a very comfortable chair in the living room and the guests would occupy the other available seats in the room. They tended to move the chairs often, in order to be closer to Dad. Mom, on the other hand, would be in the kitchen with the visiting women and she carried on all kinds of conversations with them. She would soon make sure that she had coffee or tea and some snacks available for their visitors.

The visitors, who came, seemed to really love their visits whether their visit was with either Mom or Dad, or at times, with both of them. My Dad was always loaded with information and was able to tell all kinds of stories about the visitors' relatives and/or friends. Dad was like a big book of knowledge and he could tell the visitors on numerous occasions stories that the visitors never heard before. Often Dad could take a number of visitors back in time when the visitors, themselves, were just youngsters. Dad, on many occasions, would add a lot of humour to his stories.

After telling the visitors many stories, Dad took a well-deserved break from his storytelling. When he took his self-made break, Dad would ask his visitors to be quiet and when this quietness came about, Pop's visitors would hear sounds coming from Dad, as he recited from memory, verses of the Qur'an, the holy book of the Muslims. His recitations filled the room as the visitors, themselves, quietly said their own recitations from the holy book.

The reciting of the verses would go on for ten to fifteen minutes and Dad would then announce that he was finished reciting the verses. My Dad would then ask the visitors what else they would like to know. The new stories would continue for a short while longer and Dad would then say to the visitors, "Let's go to the kitchen for some food," which Mom had prepared.

Mom would be ready for them as they paraded into the kitchen where each person took a seat at the table. My Mother must have had the strength of a superperson in order to prepare good-tasting food on so many different occasions for a number of different people. Sometimes, however, when preparing her food, my Mom would be helped by a short, skinny Lebanese woman by the name of Lila Tarrabain. Lila wasn't completely fluent in the English language, but she was fluent enough in order for our family members to have a very good understanding of what she was communicating. She, also, was very fluent in the Arabic language so this made it possible for Dad and her to communicate with each other without any problems at all taking place.

Lila, herself, was an excellent cook when it came to making Arabic food. Either she would help Mom make a lot of the food in our kitchen or she would bring some of the food over to our house from her own home, which was located about one block down the street from where we lived. When I was around in our home during those days of "good food-eating", my memory now brings back the Kibbee that Lila made and would often bring it freshly-fried to our house. Kibbee, according to my understanding is like a national food for the countries of Lebanon and Syria.

Kibbee, usually, was made in a football shape or a round patty shape. Its ingredients were crushed wheat. (known to the Lebanese as bulgar or smeed). When the bulgar rested in water, the grains would swell in size and become soft. At this point, with the water drained from it, the bulgar was mixed with some lean ground beef, along with onions and salt added to it. All of the ingredients would be mixed by hand and then small amounts of it would be shaped into the football and/or patty shapes. As each Kibbee was being shaped, a meat mixture or a meat and nut mixture would be worked into the centre of either of the Kibbee's two shapes. The raw Kibbee shapes would then be fried in a hot oil. They were and still are excellent to eat while still a bit hot. They are, also, very delicious to eat on the cold side. My Mom, as well as Lila Tarrabain, also, was a great Kibbee maker and whenever Lila and Mom worked together, they could do a lot of Kibbee in a very short time period.

Another dish that Lila often brought to our house was a soft, creamy cheese dish, known as labna. Of course, it would be made with milk that was boiled and then cooled to a medium-warmth. A bacteria mix would then be added to the milk that had been cooled and then a cover would be placed on top of the pot and, then, the pot, with the milk in it, would be wrapped in a blanket. The wrapped pot with the milk mixture, would, usually, sit overnight on the counter. In the morning, the blanket and the top of the pot would be removed and Lo! and behold the milk mixture would now be much thicker. Lila would then scrape the top of the mixture and then placed the scraped mixture into a small-sized jar so that it could be used as a starter for the next batch of labna that was going to be made. The thickened milk mixture that remained in the pot was stirred and you could eat it as it was. Some people, when eating it, loved to add salt and pepper to the dish in order to enhance its taste. At this stage, the mixture, which is now slightly thickened is known as laban.

In order to harden the laban a lot more, but still keeping it in a softened condition, where it turns into the cheese, you have to place the laban into a certain type of cloth bag and then let the whey (liquid) drain out of the bag which is now in a hanging position. The whey is collected in a container that is placed below the bag. In time, only the soft cheese will remain in the bag and, at this point, the cheese becomes known as labna. This labna is one of the best-tasting cheese that many people love to have on their plate. Labna is great when you put it onto a home-made piece of Syrian/Lebanese bread. This bread was another food product that Lila was an expert at making. Often, after she made the bread in her own oven at home, she would bring it over to our house, along with some labna. In order to make things look like a little meal, we would have some nice Kalamata olives ready to eat along with some turnips that were mixed with beets. The mixture of turnips and beets allowed for the turnips to end up with a light red colour and still it maintained the turnip's taste.

Mom, also, made her Arab food specialty which was known as fatayer. The fatayer is, usually, made with a round piece of dough which has a filling placed on it. The filling can be a mixture of lean beef with salt, pepper and onions added to the meat. A spinach mixture, as well as a potato mixture can, also, be placed on the rounded dough piece. Each mixture is placed in the centre of the dough and then the dough parts are brought together by squeezing different parts of it with the fingers so that the mixture is completely covered by the squeezed dough. The fatayers are then placed on a pan and put in a warm oven and kept there until the fatayers are a strong golden brown in colour. After the fatayers are baked, they are removed from the oven and then, graciously, brushed with butter, margarine or oil. Once the fatayers cooled off, they were ready to enjoy just on their own with no other added dishes. Each fatayer was like a meal on its own. How many a person might eat at any time depended on how hungry the individual was. Not only was my mother excellent at doing the fatayers, she, also, had great skills in making Kibbee. In addition, because of her Ukrainian heritage, Mom was able to make great perogies and terrific plum dumplings.

When my mother, bless her soul, was diagnosed with liver cancer in 1964, I realized that her life would soon come to an end in the not too far future. At that point, I understood even though her coming death would mean that I and other family members would have to show a lot of strength in dealing with the days ahead which, eventually, would see her taken from Dad and all of the other family members. When Mom was at home during those days, I made sure that I communicated with her in such a way that quite often would result in me shedding numerous and what seemed to be endless tears. Even though tears would roll down my face, at times, I knew that I couldn't have my Mom seeing me cry. I tried my hardest at all times to hide those tears from my beloved Mother and, needless to say, it was a really tough time for me to cope with.

As I ate with Mom over her remaining days, I tried to carry on various conversations with her. Some of those conversations centred around getting her recipes for the great food that she always made. Even though I found it kind of tough getting those recipes from Mom, I was able to do it without her being aware as to why I wanted the recipes. However, there were times that my Mother questioned me about why I wanted to know so much about her recipes and I simply had to lie to her by saying that I might be a cook some day and that I would like to use her recipes in my cooking. She seemed to have gone along with what I was saying at that time. The real reason, however, as to why I wanted the recipes was that I would have them and I could use those recipes after Mom had left us. Mom would pass away on November 9th, 1964.

In my own way of thinking, I refer to my Mother's death as a rude awakening in my own life because I now knew that death could come calling whenever it wanted to and there was really little if anything, that we as individuals, could do about it. Family members who lived outside of Edmonton along with all family members who lived in the city, as well as, a great number of friends, attended her funeral. Mom's funeral service was held at the Al Rashid Mosque when it was located on 111th Avenue. My Mother's death was the first death of so many more family deaths which would follow in the years ahead.

Journey to Mecca

While mom was still living, Dad decided that he wanted to follow through on doing the fifth pillar of Islam. This pillar says that a Muslim should make the pilgrimage to Mecca if he or she can afford to do so and only if there is no hardship imposed on the family. It is an obligation only for those who are physically and financially able to perform it.

The other four pillars of Islam are:

1. There is no God worthy of worship except Allah (the Arabic word for God) and Muhammad is His messenger.
2. The Muslim has to pray five times a day at dawn, noon, mid-afternoon, sunset and nightfall. The prayers are a direct link between the worshipper and God.
3. The next pillar says that a Muslim should give alms (zakat). According to the Qur'an, all Muslims should give part of their wealth to others such as the needy, travellers, and orphans.
4. The fourth pillar involves the Fast during the holy month of Ramadan. During this holy month, individuals follow a fast where they are not allowed to eat, drink or smoke from dawn to sunset. Only after sunset, on each day of Ramadan, can the fast be broken.

After making his decision to go to Mecca, Father had some discussions with one of his cousins, whom I mentioned earlier in my writing of this story. The cousin I am talking about is Alex Amery. In Dad's discussions with Alex, my father brought up the thought of, also, going back to visit Lala in Lebanon, their home village. In addition, Dad asked Cousin Alex if he would like to make the pilgrimage to Mecca with him. Alex agreed to go with Dad to Lala, but declined the invitation to go to Mecca. It is unclear as to why Alex declined the Mecca invitation. So in mid-1960, Dad and Alex were on their way to Lala. Once they reached Lala, Dad and his cousin, Alex, would reacquaint themselves with family members and friends they hadn't seen in years. These family members and friends included some people who were now eighty years old or even older and, also, there was a big group of younger relatives who were all born while Cousin Alex and Dad were living in Canada.

Eventually, Dad and a group of people from Lala would make their way to Mecca for the pilgrimage. Alex would remain behind in Lala and he started to search for a wife. He was never married up to this time. Alex soon found a potential wife, but things did not work out for the couple.

Alex, however, continued his search for a wife. Soon, he would find a caring person, by the name of Khadija, who he married and became his mate for life. This couple would have a family of their own made up of four boys, Awid, Mahmoud, Ahmed and Mohammed. They would, also, have one daughter, Mariam, who now goes by the name of Mary. Khadija had been previously married and has several children from that marriage. When Alex and Khadija returned to Edmonton, they only brought two of those children with them. One was a son called Rafic and the other one was a daughter called Fatema. The rest of her children remained behind in Lebanon.

When the time came for Dad and his friends to leave for Mecca, they journeyed out of Lala and made their way to Beirut, Lebanon's capital city. In Beirut, they would catch a plane that took them to Mecca.

The scene in Mecca, upon their arrival, had to be a very fantastic view. Dad said that the area was packed with people who came to Mecca with the same purpose in mind as Dad and his friends and that purpose was to complete the pilgrimage. I am not going to go over all of the activities involved in Dad's trip to Mecca, but I do want to point out that one night Dad was sleeping in a tent with his friends.

This tent was held in place by a set of wooden pegs with ropes attached to them, and, as well, the ropes would be tied to the tent itself. There were a number of pegs and ropes which kept the canvas of the tent in place. During the dark hours of one evening, Dad had to get up in order to go to the bathroom. As he got out of the tent and then moved around in the darkness, he suddenly tripped over one of the pegs and fell to the ground. His body then started to roll along the hilly ground for several minutes. Dad then yelled for help and his friends moved out of the tent, very carefully, and were on their way to rescuing him. One of his friends carried some sort of light which lit up the darkness. They soon were on the path which led them to Dad. When they reached Dad, he was yelling with pain. Dad pointed to his hip area and told his friends how painful the hip was. A doctor, who was now in the area confirmed that Dad had what appeared to be a broken hip. The question now arose as to what was going to happen next. After some discussion, the group agreed that they were going to continue on with the pilgrimage rather than return to Lala. Even, Dad, suffering through his pain was in favour of continuing on with the pilgrimage. But how was Dad to continue on with the journey, which now had his hip in some type of cast? His friends, as a group, exhibited a very clever way of thinking in order to ensure that there would be a very successful pilgrimage, not only for Dad, but for all of his friends, as well. They decided to place Dad on a stretcher and then carried Dad and the stretcher around the Ka'aba the required number of times. Dad never told me if he completed all of the necessary steps of the pilgrimage, but knowing him well, along with the strength of his determination, he probably completed whatever he was capable of doing. His friends exhibited what we may say went way beyond the call of duty in helping one of their friends achieve that which didn't seem to be achievable. Unfortunately, one of Dad's friends would not live to see the happy ending of Dad's pilgrimage because that friend died before the pilgrimage was completed.

After completing the pilgrimage, Dad was taken to a hospital in Saudi Arabia, for treatment and a much-needed recovery period. His friends were able to contact us in Edmonton and told us about Dad's pilgrimage accident, as well as providing us with information about the recovery he was going through in Saudi Arabia. At this point, in time, our family had to come to some type of agreement as to how we were going to help Dad out. The two oldest brothers, Alex and Mickey, would lead the family discussions and through these discussions, they would come up with an answer as to how we would get our father back to Edmonton.

The discussions which took place centred around our sister, Emily, who worked for the World Bank in Washington, D.C. Emily agreed that she would do as much as she could in order to ensure that Dad got back to his Edmonton home. First of all, the World Bank agreed to give Emily time off so that she could work on Dad's return. Next, she got in touch with two Saudi Arabian princes, who she knew quite well and asked them for their assistance. They agreed to help out as much as they possibly could. The princes would then find the hospital Dad was in and went to visit him. They, then, in turn made the arrangements to get Dad back to Beirut. Things worked out smoothly, but I have no idea as to whom paid for Dad's airfare to Beirut as well as his hospital bill in Saudi Arabia. Our family had much to be thankful for when it came to the kindness that was shown by the two princes along with Emily's unselfish kindness. Once Dad landed in Beirut, a vehicle was made available by our relatives in Lala, and Dad and Emily were taken by that vehicle back to the home of one of his nephews, in whose house, he would spend several months for his recovery period. The family, in Edmonton, and Emily, who was now back in Washington, kept in close contact with our Lala relatives.

When our family felt that Dad had made a strong enough recovery, it was decided that Emily, once again, would lead the way in getting Dad back to Edmonton. Our sister, Emily, then took more time off from work at the World Bank and she now was able to make arrangements to go to Beirut and then on to Lala in order to see Dad. She would stay in Lala for several weeks and worked on arranging to get Dad back to his home in Edmonton. Emily was, undoubtedly, a very smart person and it wouldn't be long before we would be greeting Dad back home in Edmonton. At this time, Pop was being moved around in a wheelchair. After his return home, Dad had to have another operation on the hip that was broken, and when that operation was completed, Dad would return to the home he was away from for a good length of time. When he arrived home, our father was able to enjoy the numerous members of his family as well as his many friends who came to visit him.

My Sister Emily

Emily, in my opinion, played a great role in prolonging Dad's life. When I think about my family members, I have great admiration for

Emily because she was not only a great sister, but was, also, a good friend who was blessed with much kindness. My sister, Emily, passed away on May 2nd, 1978.

The start of Emily's bad days came while she was on a mission for the World Bank in Africa. One day, while walking, Emily tripped and fell to the ground and from that fall she felt a certain amount of pain. She, then, went to the doctor to get a checkup. An examination revealed that she had breast cancer. Over the next few years, the breast cancer would grow and, eventually, that cancer would turn into bone cancer and it would not be long before the first of our family's children would have her life taken from us. I remember, sitting with Dad, in the living room, at home, on the day of Emily's death. I saw many tears flowing from Dad's eyes as he pounded his head with his right fist and he said to me, "Why didn't Allah take his life first, before taking any of his children's lives?" I remained silent and put my arms around him and held him close to me with a big hug.

I will never forget how kind Emily was to me, her youngest brother. While on one of her missions in Africa, she invited me to visit her there. For some unknown reason, I turned down her kind offer. When I think back to that invitation, I can now sincerely say that I made one great big mistake turning down Emily's invitation.

Throughout certain periods of our lifetimes Emily and I established an excellent communication relationship where we would write to each other on a regular basis. After, she would send me information from the place she was at, whether that information be handwritten or in the form of some type of souvenir such as stamps, airplane menus or small collector's items. When I was attending university, she would always ask me if I needed financial assistance. I would insist that I didn't need the financial help, but one time she sent me a cheque for $700.00 and told me to spend it wisely on my educational needs.

With all of the neat things I received from Emily, my thinking ability started to climb to a higher level. My level of thinking now went from a local, narrow type of thinking all the way to an international level of thinking. Her help in getting me to think at a higher, worldly level, undoubtedly, shaped my thinking for the rest of my life. Emily used to return to Edmonton at least once a year and when she was at home with the family, it was always enjoyable to carry on an exchange of our thoughts as we sat together during those unforgettable days. I, also, have a number of letters that I saved over the years when she sent them to me.

Emily was considered to be an excellent photographer whose pictures and slides won her much acclaim in the section she worked at of the World Bank. She, also, climbed Mount Kilimanjaro, about 5900 metres high, on one of her African missions.

When Emily was diagnosed with the breast cancer, she returned to Washington, for treatment. During this time, I decided to go to Washington to be with her, and, hopefully, I could bring some comfort to her while I was there. She would remain in Washington after I returned home, but as the months passed by, things grew a lot tougher for her. She would, eventually, be visited by my older brothers, Alex and Teddy. Their intention for the visit was to make arrangements, with Emily's agreement, to bring her back to Edmonton in order to be with other family members. Upon her arrival in Edmonton, she would stay at the house with Dad, Lila and myself. However, as her condition worsened over the following weeks, she would now become a patient at the Royal Alex Hospital in order to receive the care she now required. When I went to see her one afternoon, after I finished my teaching for the day, I noticed blood coming down one side of her mouth. It was at this time, I had the feeling that she didn't really have that much more time to live. My sister, Emily, would pass away not long after my visit on that day, a day I wished never existed in our family's life. At the cemetery, she would be buried next to our Mother.

Dad Passes Away

In 1979, the next tragedy would strike. This time, it would be our dearly, beloved father who would pass away. From the time of Emily's passing and my Dad's death on November 3rd, 1979, my father would have to deal with his prostate cancer. During this period of his life, he remained at the family's home living with Lila and myself. It should be noted that after our Mother passed away on June 21st, 1964, Lila and I took over all responsibilities for caring for our father. The two of us devoted our future years to being with Dad and as a result, Lila and myself never got married up to this time. I, however, would, eventually, marry in 1988, nine years after Dad had passed away.

I remember the day Dad passed away and it continues to be very vividly entrenched in my mind. That day, the rains came pouring down, like I never saw before. It made me wonder if God was opening up the heavens in order to accept Dad who was, in my opinion, a very great person here on Earth.

Lila, Other Family Members and Me

Life for me would be different after the passing of Dad. No longer would I be making coffee and supper for him. The house became quite a bit lonely for me without Dad being around. I would return to school and on numerous nights in the home, I would stay awake until one or two o'clock in the morning marking my students' work and working on lesson plans for the coming days of teaching. Many of those nights continued to be quite lonely and I would be lying if I told you that I didn't have many tearful nights during that time period.

In those days, my sister, Lila, was gone from the house. Each week she would leave for Calgary in order to help look after the family business there. Lila would help our brother, Eddie, at the business and she, in turn, would have a very reliable assistant named Doreen. Each weekend, Lila returned to Edmonton and would spend time with me as well as going out with her friends.

As for me, after Dad passed away, I started to get more involved in various activities. I became President of the Edmonton Multicultural Society and in our school system, I would become the President of the Greater Edmonton Teachers' Convention Association (GETCA) and was in charge of a group that planned a two day convention for approximately six thousand teachers.

During those days, I often thought of my mother, my sister, Emily, and, of course, my father. My mind would constantly keep thinking about Dad and the great, enjoyable walks we had where we told each other those fantastic family stories. I knew that it was impossible to bring Dad back to life, but I, also, realized that he and I could still go out for those great walks we had over the years, knowing full well that Dad would now be walking by my side, in memory only. So with Dad walking alongside of me, in my imagination, I, or should I say, we, started once again to walk along the path we just used in our travels so many years ago.

I walked, quite slowly, on that first day after I decided to continue following the path Dad and I used so often. My story on this day brought back memories of my family. As stated earlier, we had eighteen children in our family. There were two younger brothers, however, who passed away when they both were less than a few years old. Sixteen of us survived including Mom, Dad, eight brothers and six sisters. Today (2019) only four of the original family members remain living—my brothers Sine, Jimmy and myself are the only brothers remaining while my sister, Lila, is the only surviving sister. Although it is very difficult for me to think about all of the family members who have passed away, this part of the story must, also, be told. These are the family members who have left us up to this time.

1. My brother, Alex, the oldest family member, passed away from Alzheimer's. He had this illness for several years before he died. He, along with our brother, Mickey, started the family businesses.
2. Mickey, the second oldest brother, would die from a type of cancer.
3. Emily, as mentioned earlier, died from bone cancer.
4. Lily passed away in Fort Wayne, Indiana. I am not certain as to what she died from.
5. My sister, Zina, also, passed away from cancer and died in Fort Wayne, Indiana, as well.

6. My brothers, Eddie and Teddy, were twins. Eddie died in Calgary while Teddy passed away in Edmonton. Both of these brothers are buried at the Muslim section of the Beechmount Cemetery in Edmonton.
7. Our sister, Mona, died in Winnipeg, Manitoba.
8. Minnie, our eldest sister, passed away in Edmonton.
9. My brother, Kemal, had colon cancer and died in Edmonton.

In addition to these family members passing away, there were many of our friends and relatives from the community who would be lost over the years. On the one hand it is so sad to think about the loss of these close friends and family members, but on the other hand it is a great feeling to know how much these same people contributed not only to my life but to so many other lives as well.

As I continued to walk that path with Dad, in my thoughts, I began to think about Alex and my other brothers and sisters. Alex, the oldest of the children was a very business-oriented person. He knew how to run a business properly and he had many outstanding communicational skills. In addition, to the business skills, he possessed, he was, also, a strong social activist. Alex was always concerned about what was happening in our city and when he thought something wasn't being done properly, he either would be on the phone to a city department or he would be writing a letter to the editor of the Edmonton Journal in order to express his concerns. He and his brother, Mickey, worked together helping candidates whenever elections took place. It did not matter if the elections were being held federally, provincially or municipally. With the help of Mickey and Alex several candidates they supported were elected during those elections. Alex would marry June McLennan and the two would have a couple of children. Bonnie would be the first one to be born and Ian would be born after Bonnie. Ian would pass away from multiple sclerosis when he was in his early fifties. Bonnie is still living and has made her home in Hawaii for many years.

Mickey was my second oldest brother. He, too, was a person who had a great business mind. In addition, Mickey was involved in politics as well as being more actively involved in social activities than Alex was.

He would join clubs like the Kinsmen and he became an elected member of an exhibition board known as Northlands. Mickey worked his way up to a position where he was in charge of organizing the annual exhibition parade for several years. He was a very generous person and whenever he saw people in need, he would help them out as much as possible. Although I can't say if he was a strong, religious person, I can, honestly, state that he believed in the religion of Islam and whenever possible he would go to the mosque and pray on Fridays. After the prayers, he would bring several of the pioneer Muslims over to Mom's and Dad's house.

I remember being home on many of those days because on Friday afternoons, I didn't have any university classes. When the "oldtimers" such as Uncle Sam Jamha, Alex Darwish, Mike Tarrabain and Alex Hamilton came, I would sit and listen, carefully, to their conversations. The conversations were usually in English, but, they, also, spoke a lot of Arabic, as well. When they talked in Arabic, I would be a bit lost because I couldn't speak or understand the language. I was, however, able to pick up some Arabic words which gave me some idea as to what they were talking about when those words came up in their conversations.

Mickey was married to Evelyn McQuillan and they had five children, three of whom were the girls Patty, Linda and Cindy. Jeff and Donald were the names of the two boys.

One year, a young relative of ours from Lala, by the name of Mohammed Amery arrived in Edmonton. He stayed with our father, Lila and myself. Mickey spent a lot of time in helping Mohammed out with his educational programming and providing him with numerous clothing items at no cost. Mohammed Amery, in time, would be elected to the Alberta Legislature and would be one of Alberta's longest serving elected members over the years. Mickey's generosity in helping others is remembered today by a number of people. I have already talked about Emily who worked at the World Bank, but I forgot to mention that she always phoned home so that she could speak to the family members on many different occasions. These phone calls was one of her ways of always ensuring that she was keeping in touch with not only Mom and Dad, but, also, her brothers, sisters and even some family friends at times.

Out of all of the family members that I probably knew least about was my sister, Lily. One of the reasons why I didn't know that much about her is that Lily didn't really come to Edmonton that often. She married when I was quite young and she and her husband, Joe, made their home in the United States. Whenever she and Joe made visits to Edmonton, Lily always proved herself to be a very jovial person. She had a very strong laugh that could be heard a distance away from where she was. She, also, tended to be what I would call a heavy cigarette smoker. Out of all of our family members, I believe, without any doubt at all, that Lily was always the most jovial around people. Lily and Joe had two children by the names of Joel and Karen. Both of the children and their families now make their home in Fort Wayne, Indiana.

Zina was a sister who lived in the same city, Fort Wayne, as Lily did but it seems as if there were times when the two sisters didn't communicate very well with each other. My sister, Zina, really loved the outdoors. Often she would go and soak herself in the sunshine. She would get a very dark suntan from staying in the sun so much. I can't say for certain if all of this sunshine led to the cancer that she would die from. She was married to Byron Emrich and the couple had two girls, Cherlene and Carla. Cherlene died at a very young age and I believe she died from diabetes. I haven't heard anything from Carla in many years and I don't know what, if anything, has taken place in her life up to this time.

While living in Fort Wayne, Zina had a Lebanese neighbor who was the aunt of the movie and television star, Jamie Farr. Jamie starred in the popular television series M.A.S.H. His first movie part came in the movie "Blackboard Jungle". When his name appeared in the movie's credits, he would be known as Jameel Farah. On several occasions, Jamie Farr would come to Edmonton to star in plays at a theatre known as Stage West which was located in a hotel by the name of the Mayfield Inn.

When Jamie appeared at his first play in Edmonton, I asked my sister, Zina, if she would talk to Jamie's aunt in order to see if Jamie would be willing to meet a few of us after his performance. Jamie, being the friendly person that he was, agreed to meet us and on that evening, he gave us about an hour of his time, after the show. In addition, I asked Jamie if he would like to come to the house to meet the rest of the family and a few of our friends. He agreed to come and early that evening, on the day he came, I went to pick Jamie up at the hotel where he was staying and then I brought him to the family house. We had a very enjoyable evening on that once in a lifetime occasion. Also, I can always boast that I drove one of the stars of the hit television series, M.A.S.H. at the time, in my car, on that particular day, in order to bring him to the house.

On other occasions when Jamie Farr came to Edmonton to again perform at Stage West, several family members, including my wife, Soraya, and myself would go and see the play that he was in and I would make arrangements for us to always meet him after his show was finished. Although our relationship wasn't really that strong, I will say that it was a very friendly one and that Jamie always showed much kindness to us on the evenings we met after the completion of his shows.

Unfortunately, the last time Jamie appeared in Edmonton, he became sick and the rest of his performances had to be cancelled. He never has returned to Edmonton to perform since that time.

My brother, Ted, or Teddy as I preferred to call him, came with us to see Jamie Farr at the Stage West Theatre. Teddy, as noted earlier was a fraternal twin to my brother, Eddie.

Teddy was a fun-loving person. He was the one who did some exaggerating in order to make his stories more enjoyable to listen to. This brother was really expressive in telling his stories and sometimes, as his stories unravelled, it became hard for his listeners to separate what was real, from those parts of the stories and what was exaggerated. Often his stories were told with lots of laughter in them. I remember when I was growing up, Ted and his friends were always going out at night. He would return home at different hours of each of those nights and would open the unlocked back door of the house very quietly so that no one could hear him coming in. In those earlier days, Mom and Dad never locked the doors because they weren't worried about strangers coming into the house as uninvited guests. Life was different in those days which now seems to be so far, far away and are, forever, shoved into the years of the past. There was one night when Teddy came home, and Dad was sitting in the kitchen. Brother Ted never said anything to Dad at that time and instead he made his way to the fridge. He, then, opened the fridge door and took out something to eat. Dad, in a comical way said to Teddy, at that time, "Why is it that you go to the fridge first, instead of saying hello to me first?" Teddy, I was told, stood there dumbfounded and then managed to say in a humourous way, "I didn't know that you were here!"

Ted would, in time, join the family business Western Varieties. While in the business, he started to become an expert at getting to know a lot about the world of toys. He would enhance his knowledge of toys by travelling to yearly toy shows held, generally, in Toronto. In those beginning years, when going to Toronto, he would travel with a friend who also, was on his way to the toy show. As time went on, however, Teddy began to travel with one of his brothers or his sister, Lila, to these shows. After the shows were over, the two of them would journey into the United States to visit our sister, Emily, in Washington, D.C. as well as our sisters, Zina and Lily, who were in Fort Wayne, Indiana.

As the years moved on Teddy and other family members started to come up with a new idea for marketing their toys. They now started to sell wrapped presents during the Christmas season to companies in various provinces as well as in Canada's northern territories. The presents wouldn't only be wrapped, they would, also, be labelled into boys and girls gifts along with the ages the presents were for. Later on, each company was asked to supply the name of each person who would receive a gift along with their ages. This type of labelling tended to make each gift more personal. Most companies, from that time on, would use this type of labelling, but some companies, usually, bigger ones, kept using the boy-girl labels with the ages included on each label. All gifts were sold at wholesale prices and the giftwrapping and labelling were free of any charge.

Each year, Ted and his staff would set up a toy show in order to entice customers to purchase their presents. In order to get the companies to come into the yearly Toy Show at the Western Varieties' location and place an order, the toys would be displayed and unwrapped on several walls for viewing purposes by the buying companies' representatives.

The toy display would be set up in early April and letters were sent out to the companies inviting their representatives, starting around May

16th of each year to come in and pick their Christmas presents. A lot of the required toys chosen were estimated numbers, but Ted would put these estimated numbers away until the final numbers were received, usually, several weeks before the company's Christmas party took place. Because of the great organization of these pre-arranged activities, there really were very few problems in the way the Christmas orders were done. Most companies were very pleased with the service provided for their Christmas parties and this service brought most companies back year after year to purchase their Christmas presents.

When I started working at Western Varieties, after my retirement from other businesses, I would help Ted with setting up the toy show display and dealing with the companies by trying to get them to place an order all the way to getting the labels ready to place on each present. A person, as well, was hired to type up the labels.

Things worked out very well over the years until Ted got sick. Ted's sickness would have him placed in the hospital for several weeks. Others, at the wholesale, would help to replace the work Ted usually did until he could return. Ted, eventually, returned but was limited to the work that he was now capable of doing. Several months would pass while Ted worked on his recovery, after which he resumed most of his duties. There is no doubt that Ted really loved working on the Christmas presents and he was so happy whenever he was able to greet all of the great people who came into the wholesale from the various companies over the years.

Ted's sickness was a kidney problem. Over the years, he had to go to the hospital three times each week for dialysis. He often drove himself to the hospital on the days of dialysis. When things got really tough on Ted, one of his children took him to dialysis. As time went on, the doctors wanted to do what they considered to be a minor operation for Ted. This minor operation, however never worked out and it is from that operation that Ted's life would come to an end. Teddy's death was a sad time for the family members, but what can any family do when death comes calling? Before Teddy had his operation, the family had sold the Western Varieties Wholesale business in 2009 and this sale seemed to have made life so much easier to deal with when any sickness came rolling along.

Our brother, Eddie, was a fraternal twin to Teddy. The twins got along very well and in their early lives, these two brothers got into a fair amount of trouble with the police. Looking after these trouble situations probably drove Mom and Dad crazy at times. Eddie, I think was more of a troublemaker than Ted. Eddie's troubles would cause him to leave home on several occasions. He, also, got into some fights at times and the fights would lead to trouble with the police. Dad and Mom would make their journeys to the police station more than just a few times in order to get Eddie out of jail. Things were made easier for Mom and Dad, at times, because several police officers took a liking to our family. On the other hand, however, maybe the officers just wanted to make sure that some family characters wouldn't be permanent fixtures, just hanging around, uninvited, at the police station.

Previously, I mentioned that Eddie became an employee with Mr. Weisler's company. He, eventually, in time, worked his way up to the running of the family business in Calgary. While in Calgary, Eddie developed a growing desire to bring about a very successful life for himself. In addition to running the family's Calgary business, Eddie took many chances which would drive him onto the road of success. He got to know numerous people very well and a number of these people would, eventually, partner up with Eddie and they would begin to buy real estate properties, shopping centres and some restaurants. One of the restaurants he became a partner in was a Tony Roma restaurant, which is a company known for its ribs. Several of the shopping centres were anchored by 7-11 stores. He would own condominiums in Hawaii, as well.

In the beginning, Eddie had an excellent relationship with his partners, but as time went on a number of these relationships would begin to sour for a variety of reasons. The partners would now start to buy out other partners and after the sell-offs, the partners tended to travel their separate ways. Sometimes the relationships among the partners grew so harsh, where the partners would not even communicate with each other for several years and in some cases that communication ended forever. Eddie, however, did maintain his relationships with some partners and they continued to work on building up their business ventures.

My brother, Eddie, was always kind to me. I remember that he bought a car for me one year, while I was going to university. When he passed away, he would leave me some money in his will so that I could pay off the mortgage on our house. Eddie died in Calgary after having several car accidents. The accidents, partially, led to him having poor health over several years, and, in turn, his internal body systems were severely damaged.

Eddie, never did marry so far as I know. He seemed to have had many close relationships with several female partners over the years. Some of these relationships led to the birth of several children. Very few of his children, however, have not kept in touch with our main family members. My brother, Eddie is buried at the Muslim section of the Beechmount Cemetery in Edmonton where his grave lies alongside other family members. I believe that two of his children, plus the woman he had lived with in Calgary over a number of years, picked out Eddie's gravestone. In my opinion, his gravestone is a disgrace. The gravestones for all other family members at the Beechmount Cemetery stand at a slight angle and they rise about two feet into the air. Eddie's gravestone, on the other hand is rather on the small size and is sitting flat, at ground level. What is sad about his stone is that people can walk over it throughout the warmer months of the year. There is no fence around it and it makes me feel awful that people are walking right over his grave as well as his gravestone. Hopefully, some day this situation can be rectified, but it will take some leadership on the part of two of his children, Mardi and Jamal, to help with the problem, previously, mentioned.

My sister, Mona, left home when she got married to Barney Loftson of Winnipeg, Manitoba. Mona was partially blind and like I said earlier, in my writing, I have no idea as to how she lost some of her eyesight. Mona always remained a happy person on most occasions and she had numerous friends who she could always depend on. At the time when she got a bit older, the CNIB (Canadian National Institute for the Blind) used to operate some small businesses located in some bigger buildings around Edmonton. Mona was in charge of one of those businesses where she was able to sell items like candy, gum, and newspapers. In those days, the CNIB would depend a great deal upon the honesty of people not to take advantage of a visually-impaired person like Mona. The customer would be expected to give the proper amount of money in order to pay for the item or items which were purchased. When change had to be given, Mona would know by feeling the size of the coins how much money should be returned to the customers. I can't say for certain how a person, like Mona, would have handled the return of money if paper currency was given to her for purchases made.

After Mona was married, she and her husband, Barney, moved to Winnipeg. They would have a family which consisted of three boys, Rick, David and Loren and one girl whose name was Mona Lynne. Each summer, Mona would bring herself and the four children to Edmonton. Barney, however, very seldom came to Edmonton with his family at that time. He would remain behind in Winnipeg during Mona's vacation period.

When coming to Edmonton, Mona and the children would travel by train. How Mona was able to look after the four children, especially when they were of a very young age, leaves me, touched, with much admiration for her and her ability to travel all the way from Winnipeg with little or no assistance. When Mona arrived in Edmonton, she would settle in at the house for several days and she, then, phoned her friends to let them know that she would like to see them. On many occasions, I would take Mona and the children to the friends' houses or the friends would come to the house to visit.

Once again, I had the opportunity to meet a whole new group of people who enhanced my life as I got to know these new friends. When Mona started to visit Edmonton during these times, I was the only person along with my sister, Lila, and Dad who were left at home. Lila, at the time, didn't know how to drive, so that is why I became the main person transporting Mona and her family. Mona would continue to return to Edmonton for a number of years. As her own family got older, there came a time when she decided to stop her return trips to Edmonton. In order to keep in touch with Dad, while he was still alive, Lila and myself and Mona would always exchange Christmas presents. Along with the exchanges that took place, Mona, each year would send us her famous Icelandic cake during this festive time of the year. Also, Mona made sure that on her visits to Edmonton that she had the Icelandic cake available as a treat for the family.

The last time, our family members in Edmonton had an opportunity to talk to Mona was several years ago when her health had deteriorated to the point where her children placed her in an extended care centre located in Winnipeg. By this time, Barney had passed away, a number of years earlier. Mona, in time, would, herself, pass away in Winnipeg with her immediate family by her side.

Minnie was my oldest sister. As mentioned earlier, she married at a young age and because of this, Dad and Minnie's husband, Charlie Joseph, just never got along over the years. Undoubtedly, Charlie's taking away of Minnie from the family, probably played a great part in what would be a silent, bitter rivalry between Dad and Charlie. I can't say for certain but I have no doubt that Dad would not talk to Charlie ever again after the marriage took place. Dad, did, however, come with me along with a few other family members, when we went to see Minnie at her house after Charlie passed away in order to pay our respects to Minnie and her family.

While married, Minnie and our Dad got along quite well most of the time, but Minnie showed some bitterness in conversations at times, when it came to discussing Charlie. I would say that Minnie stood up for Charlie more than she should have and probably she likely didn't understand Dad's views of the marriage situation as well as she should have. We really could argue for years as to whom was right and who was wrong when it comes to Minnie's married life.

After their marriage, Minnie and Charlie would open several grocery stores, some large and some small ones. I know as a matter of fact that Minnie was the main operator of each store and, as well, I believe that Charlie probably did not do his share when it came to running the stores.

I remember that one store was located in the area where I went to a Junior High School. After school was over, I would, on a number of occasions, visit Minnie. When I got to the store, she would always provide me with a bottle of Coca-Cola and then we would talk about a variety of things when no customers were around. I really enjoyed those visits because I got to know my oldest sister much more than I thought was possible. Our talks would, generally, be about those everyday topics and what was really great during those talks was that they were always argument-free.

In addition to being a good storekeeper, Minnie was, also, a great cook. She loved to make pastries and I was, extremely pleased, when she gave me some to take home. In addition, to making the pastries, Minnie had very good knowledge when it came to making certain Arab foods such as Kibbee and fatayer. Eventhough I am much older now, I still have many fond memories of visiting Minnie at her store and recalling all of the great and enjoyable talks we had. I, also, cannot forget the delicious foods she would feed me as well. Minnie passed away in Edmonton.

The next family member I want to tell you about is my brother, Sine. He is the third youngest of the brothers. Sine is and always has been an independent sort of character, as long as I can remember. He is a person who likes to joke quite a bit and he shows this joking behavior when he is in a crowd. His jokes are quite funny at times, but at other times it is hard for me to say that there is real humour in some of the jokes. No matter what, I laugh at nearly all of Sine's jokes in order to not hurt his feelings. I don't really know if other family members or even if Sine's own children see his jokes in the same way that I do. A number of Sine's jokes are aimed at the politicians. Politically, Sine appears to be a very right-leaning Conservative. Myself, on the other hand, is a very strong Liberal supporter. Needless to say, whenever family gatherings took place, Sine and I would try to egg each other on when politics were introduced at the gatherings. Sine, myself and others would always enjoy those political discussions and we would never let things get out of hand. On my part, if I didn't like the way the political discussions were headed, I would, quietly, slide a new topic onto the discussion floor and usually others would become part of the new talks which gradually became the dominant talk as the minutes ticked away. In these political discussions we would never let them heat up to a point where we got upset with each other.

Sine was the first of our family to go to university. I can't say for certain what his first year of studies was about, but I can say without any question that, eventually, he started to work on a Bachelor of Education degree. He graduated with his education degree from the University of Alberta in Edmonton.

In the mid-1960's, Sine would meet his future wife, Verna Johnson and they would marry on July 1st, 1968. Sine and Verna who, also, was a teacher would have four children. Their names are Troy, Cory, Kelly and Krista.

Sine would spend a lot of his married life working in the teaching profession and, eventually, he would get involved in the buying and renovating of houses. In addition, he would become a property manager and looked after shopping centres that our brother Eddie had partial ownership in.

After Sine retired from teaching and began purchasing and fixing houses as well as having the property management job these now became part of his everyday life. Sine, also, loved to work around his own house and always was experimenting with new garden ideas. He is, extremely, proud of the grapes that he grows in his backyard and quite often will turn the grape supply into some type of wine and jelly. Sine and his wife, Verna, continue to make their home in Edmonton.

My brother, Jim, is another family member I must tell you about. Jim is probably the hardest family member for me to write about because he and I were at an age difference where I didn't hang around him that much and, as well, he didn't hang around me because of my youthful age.

I remember, Jim, hanging out with a group of friends who would be involved with the game of baseball. At one time, our family lived in the area of the city which had a ballpark located only one block away from where our house was. Jim worked at the ballpark which was named Renfrew Ball Park, at the time. I have no idea how this park got its name, but I have a feeling that the park is named after a Lord Renfrew who was a British historical figure connected somehow to our Canadian history. Anyway, Jim and our other brothers had the job of being groundkeepers which meant that they had the responsibility of getting the baseball diamond ready for any ballgame that was going to be played. Whenever it rained, all of the groundkeepers had to pull canvas tarps out in order to cover the dirt areas of the ball diamond. These tarps would protect the dirt areas from getting muddy and thus allowed for a game to be played as soon as the rains disappeared. If the dirt somehow remained muddy, future games would be cancelled until the grounds were ready once again for games to resume. I, vaguely, remember that gasoline in big sealed barrels would be spread over any wet dirt and then the gasoline would be lit with a match and the dirt would undergo a drying process from the heat of the gasoline.

In addition to working at the ballpark, Jim was a postman for a time and he delivered mail from house to house. As well, Jim became a milkman who delivered milk that was in a wagon pulled by a horse. I can't say with any certainty, however, if his wagon was pulled by one or two horses. Jim, undoubtedly, had trouble with his wagon when he and his wagon had to travel up and down a number of hills located in his delivery area.

As Jim got older, his brothers, Mickey and Alex had opened Western Varieties Wholesale. My brother, Jim, then became a salesman for the wholesale. In the beginning years, he would make most of his sales in the Edmonton area and later on he would start covering a much wider area for his sales. He would now travel the Northern Alberta area and even went on to Yellowknife, in the Northwest Territories. His sales, also, would take him to Whitehorse in the Yukon Territory. Jim or Jimmy (as I quite often called him) seemed to have loved his days of travelling which always gave him the opportunity of meeting many new people and at the same time allowed him to make his sales to the storekeepers. His sales, undoubtedly, helped Western Varieties to grow in business over the years. Jim was an excellent salesperson according to people I have talked to.

Jim married Gwen Erickson and the couple would adopt two children, Brad and Glenda. Gwen, herself, used to be a ticket seller at a movie theatre called the Empress. Needless to say, several of my family members enjoyed sneaking into the theatre, where Gwen worked, without paying to watch not only cowboy movies but movies which would feature the Dead End Kids and the Bowery Boys. We enjoyed getting into the theatre, thanks to Gwen, free of charge. We, as a family, always agreed that Gwen was just helping out some of her future relatives by allowing them to sneak into the theatre without paying.

When Mickey and Alex left the wholesale business, Ted, Kemal, Lila and Jim would take control over a much smaller Western Varieties business and kept running it as a family business for a number of years. Eventually, some disagreements took place between Jim and the other family members and Jim's share of the business would be bought out by the three remaining partners.

Kemal (or Ken as he was known by his English name) was born after Sine and was the third youngest of the family. I don't remember too much about his younger days, but he and I, along with some older family members attended the same elementary school, called Donald Ross, which was located right across the street from our house. Because of the closeness of the school, I doubt, if any of us were ever late, for the start of the school day. There are a few things that I now am able to recall about Kemal's early life. I remember the time when some of the United States military came into Edmonton. This time period, according to Dad, was probably during the Second World War years and it was, also, the time period of the building of the Alaska Highway. The American soldiers visited the ballpark which was very close to our house and I, fondly, remember that the boxer, Joe Louis, made an appearance one particular day. I assume that Louis's appearance at the park was at the same time that the United States military visited the ballpark. There could have been a baseball game on that day, as well. Anyway, as my story unravels, there was a United States military captain by the name of Wayne Cook who saw Kemal at the ballpark and took a liking to him. Captain Cook, along with Kemal and other family members established a warm relationship at the time and the relationship lasted for a number of years. I don't recall what happened to Captain Cook other than when he passed away a letter from someone in the United States came to our house, and information in that letter gave our family the sad news that the military captain had passed away. This was a very sad period of much sorrow for our family members and it was extremely sad for my brother, Kemal.

While Captain Cook was alive, he would always write letters to Kemal. As Ken grew older and as those years progressed into the future, he began to spend more time at the ballpark. Eventually, a person by the name of John Ducey took control of the ballpark. He hired a number of local area boys to do the work required at the park. One of Ducey's favourite employees was our brother, Kemal. John Ducey, however, never called Kemal by his real name and instead always called him by the nickname of Emo. Why Ducey called Kemal, Emo, is to this day beyond my understanding. At the park, Kemal would have the position of ball boy. It would be his job, during a baseball game to hand the balls to the umpire who was positioned behind the catcher calling the balls and strikes and yelling out loud to a batter at times, "You're out!" Kemal, himself, would be quite a distance behind the catcher and umpire, seated in a chair made of metal and behind my brother would be a very high screen which protected the fans from being hit by any foul balls.

I don't ever remember having any arguments with Kemal in our younger days. He would, eventually, finish high school and then went on to university for a short time. During his first year of university, he tried his luck in the Faculty of Dentistry. Unfortunately, Kemal's days at university were few in number. He gave up on his desire to be a dentist after one year and then gave up on university altogether. Kemal would now try his luck at getting a job in the wider, outside world.

He first tried his hand at becoming an insurance agent, but this job just wasn't the type of work he wanted for a lifetime. Once again, Western Varieties would come into a family member's life and Kemal would soon be learning the techniques required to be successful in the wholesale business. At the wholesale, Kemal was a very dedicated worker and worked his way up to a position where he could buy supplies for resale to stores as well as to individuals and groups. He was very good at bargaining with the customers when the occasions ever arose. One of Kemal's weaknesses was that he could easily get frustrated with customers if they didn't bargain in good faith and, as well, when he dealt with the suppliers, some of them could, also, frustrate him. Sometimes, things became so bad in the relationships between Kemal and the customers and/or the suppliers, they would avoid each other if they were in the business area at the same time. This type of situation, definitely, was not good for Kemal along with the people he had to deal with and the overall business, in general. In time, cooler heads would prevail on all parts and all participants would be much better off so that a good business relationship could be maintained for one and all as the times kept rolling along.

Well, Dad, there really aren't too many more stories to tell about members of our family, at this time. It's undoubtedly, true that only partial information has been given for the stories we have told so far, but I hope we have picked out the highlights of each family member's story. Now it appears as if we have only two more family members stories to tell. Both of these stories are going to be about the two youngest members of our family. The first of these two stories that I am going to tell is the story of my youngest sister, and, of course, the youngest daughter of yours and our mother. This is Lila's story.

Lila was born in 1942 and still continues to live in Edmonton. Unfortunately, she never married and the reason for that is because Lila and myself devoted a number of years where we took care of you, Dad, after Mom passed away. I, however, eventually, married at a much later age after you passed away on November 3rd, 1979. Lila, for whatever reason or reasons, remained single since your departure from our lives. I know that she had a number of suitors in her life wanting to marry her, but things just didn't seem to work out. Perhaps, the men in her life, throughout the years, just were not interested in getting married for a variety of reasons. One of these reasons could have involved religious beliefs. Religion does have a way of getting involved in the lives of some people. I am not saying if this is good or bad, but it is a fact in some lives, religion plays a significant part in choices people make in their lives. As well as this religious factor, the men she was involved with might not have wanted to make their permanent home in Edmonton. Lila seemed to have loved Edmonton enough to stay here permanently for the rest of her life, instead of moving to another location, wherever that location may have been.

Lila was always a very dedicated person to the people she associated with, whether these people were family or non-family members. I, personally, thought on many occasions that my sister, Lila, was a little too dedicated to others where she tried so hard to please them. If I am right in my thinking, this type of behavior on Lila's part could have set up some sort of wall which might have prevented her from pursuing her romantic interests.

Another problem, to me, that may have influenced Lila's life was that she became very dedicated to the family business. Previously, I stated that the family had started a wholesale business in Calgary. Our brother, Eddie, was the main person who looked after the business which was called Alberta Giftwares. Eddie was a very good manager and within a few years, the business started to grow a lot. As well, Eddie, himself, was, also, into other side businesses of his own along with some friends who were his partners. In time, Eddie was very successful with his business ventures and he realized that he couldn't handle his own investments and the management of Alberta Giftwares, all at the same time. Eddie did, however, hire some people whose job was to manage the family business, but things just didn't turn out the way Eddie wanted them to be. A dilemma now existed for Eddie. So he and other family members had several discussions and the family members, Eddie included, decided to ask Lila if she would like to go to Calgary in order to help manage Alberta Giftwares. After some serious consideration, Lila decided that she would be interested in going to Calgary to help look after the business. Her decision, however, was full of hesitation because it meant that she would leave you alone, Dad, along with myself in Edmonton. I encouraged Lila to go to Calgary and I reassured her that I could look after you, Dad, as well as care for myself while she was working in Calgary.

Lila, thus, moved to Calgary, but not on a permanent basis. Her stays in Calgary would be ones where she would catch the bus on a Sunday and stay in Calgary until Friday of each week. Usually she would return to Edmonton on Fridays, late at night and, occasionally, she would come back on Saturday to be with Dad and myself. This type of arrangement would continue for numerous years and then there came a time when the family decided to shut down the Calgary business because of several reasons. The reasons included a new and expensive rental agreement for the building that the business was housed in and there was a reason much more significant to family members and that reason was that several family members had passed away. This was a factor that was hard for the remaining family members to accept. We were not used to losing family members within such a short period of time. Lila would soon return to Edmonton and then got involved in the Western Varieties business again. Western Varieties, itself, would undergo some financial difficulties and, eventually, it closes down for a short while. A few months later, Jimmy, Ted, Kemal and Lila decide to re-open Western Varieties but it would be a business now on a much smaller scale.

The new, revised Western Varieties operated by the three brothers and the one sister was built up and grew into a new thriving business that would remain in the hands of the family until they sold the business to non-family members in 2009. Lila played a great part in building up this revised Western Varieties wholesale business.

Lila now lives a retired life, but as with all of us, old age and some sickness always catches up to us. Sometimes my sister pretends that she is in good health when in reality, she is at times in poor health. She seldom will admit that her health is not as good as it should be. Dad, I keep reminding her that she should look after her own health first instead of trying to care for everyone else. But, Lila, is that type of caring person who is always there with hands outstretched in order to offer those hands to help others out. Over the years, she was the one who always put others ahead of herself. Her devotion to family was always front and centre and full of caring. Her relationships, over the years, with so many people always remained, undoubtedly, extremely strong-strong enough to have relationships that were and always will be everlasting. Well, this completes Lila's story, which is only partial in nature, and now there is only one more story to tell, Dad.

Before I start that story, Pop, I want you to know that out of our family of sixteen, only four of us remain alive today. Sine is in his early eighties and he now has devoted his life for the past several years caring for his wife, Verna, who has a type of disease we know as ALS. The disease is, also, known as Lou Gehrig's Disease. Lou Gehrig was a great baseball player for the New York Yankees and in time he passed away from the disease that is named after him. Sine has a lot of things to look after when it comes to caring for his wife. He has to take her to appointments, do a lot of work around the house and at times go to special functions. When he moves Verna into the car to travel for appointments, it takes a lot of time and effort on his part. He and Verna have had several grandchildren over the past years being added to their family.

Jimmy is another of the surviving family members and is now moving on in age. He is in his late eighties. Jim lives with his wife, Gwen, in a small-sized town called Beaumont which is not too far from Edmonton. Both Jim and Gwen tend to have a certain amount of good health, a lot of the time, but needless to say that both of them will, also, have some of those unhealthy days.

Lila still lives in the house which the family moved into in the nineteen fifties. She still lives by herself and her health is not the best at times. She continues to maintain that positive outlook on life and she keeps saying that she is healthy enough to want to keep living with her daily routine as it is. She always shows that she is a good strong fighter and even if her health knocks her down at times, she bounces back up and is ready to do battle with her bad health problems whenever the occasions arise. Lila is now battling Parkinson's Disease.

The fourth person from the family who is still living is me, your son, Richard or Richie as he was always known by family members. So now, Dad, it is time to tell a bit more about myself.

You remember, Dad, that I was born in 1939. Out of eight brothers, I was the last one to be born. When it comes down to it, I was the thirteenth born out of our family of fourteen children. In reality, though, we had a family of sixteen children. Two of our family members passed away at very young ages and are buried in Brandon, Manitoba. I don't even know what their names were. It is kind of sad not knowing the names of family members who were born and passed away at very young ages.

If we look at our family as having the fourteen children being born and having, myself, being the thirteenth born child, it wasn't really a bad omen for me. I believe that I have led a pretty good life up to the present time. I am now seventy-nine years old, in semi-good health and still active in doing things even though I have slowed down in my activities over the past few years.

When I was going to university back in the early 1960's, I remember that Mom was having some heart problems and that a Doctor Ryan came to the house and looked after her on that particular day. Doctor

Ryan recommended that Mom should go to the hospital for treatment. I cannot remember how Mom got to the hospital at that time. I believe that she stayed in the hospital on that same day, and she, also, never returned home because, in addition to the heart problem, Mom was diagnosed with liver cancer. This news was devastating for me as well as for all other family members because for the first time in my life, I would now have to live with the fact that a family member was going to die. Mom would be the first in the family to pass away and I refer to this period of my life as the rude awakening period. When Mom's life was in its final days, I remember that several brothers, myself, and my sister, Lila were told to go to the hospital. When we arrived at the hospital, we went to Mom's room and we would all say our last good-byes. When Mom died that evening, I, vividly, recall that Lila ran down the hallways of the hospital screaming and crying at the same time. A couple of us chased after her in order to quiet her down and providing her with the comfort she needed at that time.

With Mom's passing and within the very short time that followed, we soon realized that life was quite different without Mom being in our presence. When things settled down after Mom's burial, only you, Dad, along with Lila, Sine and myself were left in the house. Within a few years, Sine would marry Verna and that marriage would result in Lila, you and myself living in the house that was built for a much larger number of family members.

Mom had passed away on November 9th, 1964. I got my first university degree in the same year. It was a Bachelor of Arts degree where I majored in Sociology. There can be little doubt that it would prove to be quite hard finding a job in those days with only a Bachelor of Arts degree in Sociology. Not being able to find a job, I made the decision to go back to the University of Alberta and I registered in the Faculty of Education. I have to admit that university life was quite tough for me eventhough I would study extremely hard in order to achieve the necessary marks which would lead me to my Bachelor of Education degree in 1966. With the two degrees now packed under my feet, I went to the Edmonton Public School Board to seek a job. After some tough interviews, I was hired by the School Board and I started to teach my first class in the fall of 1966. I was assigned a grade five class in a school called Laurier Heights.

My first class, at Laurier Heights was made up of two groups. One group had a larger number and this group was considered to be made up of students who were of higher ability and, then, there was a second, smaller group, about ten in number, and this group consisted of students who had some difficulties in learning the information that was being taught.

I worked very hard during my first school year of teaching and with the help of four great teachers who got me going on the right track of my teaching career, I, eventually taught for twenty-seven years before I retired from the profession. It would be an injustice if I didn't mention the names of those four teachers who looked after me in that first teaching year. One of them was the Vice-Principal, Jim Brown, who was always there for me whenever I required some help in my everyday teaching. Orest Motowylo taught me the skills needed for setting up excellent track meets over a period of many years. Ernie Matan was another teacher who helped me out in the area of music. He was a very great music teacher. Ron Greenslade was a classroom teacher, who moved up to the position of Vice-Principal, replacing Jim Brown when Jim left the school for a new position within the Edmonton Public School Board.

My first Principal was Bill Coull. Mr. Coull was a very good principal and he was, believe it or not, my grade five teacher when he was teaching at Donald Ross School. At that time, my family lived in the Rossdale area of Edmonton where Donald Ross School was located. Bill Coull and I would cross paths on several different occasions throughout my teaching career. When I transferred from my first school, Laurier Heights, I became a grade five teacher at Scott Robertson Elementary School. The principal at Scott Robertson was none other than Bill Coull. Eventually, I made my way to Westglen Elementary School where I taught Grade Three. One of my students in one of the Grade Three classes that I taught was Bill Coull's grandson. Our world really is a very small place where the paths of people, you have known, can cross another person's path in the next chapter of his or her life.

I like to consider my first year of teaching, 1966–67, as a year that had a lot of success for me and with the awesome assistance provided for me by a number of great people, I would continue to work hard at being a teacher whom, I think, many people appreciated. I know that I might not have been successful with all of the students I taught, but on the other hand, I sincerely believe that I always tried my best to be a pretty good teacher, in the long run, for all of the students I taught.

With two months off, from teaching in 1967, because of holidays, I decided to take a vacation for nearly all of that two-month time period. I, also, can't forget that 1967 was Canada's 100th birthday and I had that unending desire to get in on some of the birthday activities that were taking place right across Canada. I had never travelled before in my lifetime up to that point, so that summer of 1967 proved to be an interesting experience for me. What did I do for my vacation in 1967?

First of all, I travelled across all of Canada except for the Northwest Territories. My travels were by bus, train, ship and airplane in order to reach any destination that was part of my itinerary. With all of these means of transportation and with all of the hotel rooms I would stay at, my nearly two-month Canadian vacation would only cost me about, believe it or not, sixteen hundred ($1600) dollars.

I started my journey out of Edmonton and travelled by Greyhound Bus to Whitehorse in the Yukon Territory. From Whitehorse, I took the narrow-gauged track train to Alaska and from there I travelled down the west coast by ship, all the way to Vancouver Island. Then it was on to Victoria and, eventually, back home to Edmonton. I only stayed in Edmonton for a few days at that time and then I started my journey eastward. I would go to Regina and see the R.C.M.P. headquarters and then I went off to Winnipeg where I took in the Pan American Games. In time I would reach Montreal where I took part in a visit to Expo '67 which Montreal was hosting that year. After leaving Montreal, I made my way to the Maritime provinces and then proceeded to St. John's, Newfoundland, Before I got to St. John's, however, I will never forget reaching Port Aux Basque, Newfoundland by ship after leaving North Sydney, Nova Scotia. My fondest memory of the trip that took me overland to St. John's was when I took the Newfie Bullet train. Riding on that Bullet train was, for me, a once in a lifetime experience. While riding the Newfie Bullet, I can, vividly, recall having a cup of coffee riding the train that day. It never occurred to me that the railway tracks were not that straight and, as well, the tracks were loaded with numerous curves along the way to St. John's. I recall that when the Bullet was taking a curved path and I had my coffee cup loaded with coffee in my hand, my coffee shot out of the cup and soaked some of the clothing that I was wearing. Like I said earlier, riding on the Bullet train was, undoubtedly, a once in a lifetime experience. A number of years later, the Newfie Bullet Train was taken out of service and a bus system replaced the train's path in the years of the future.

There were lots of highlights as I travelled across Canada in that Centennial year. Each place, I stopped at, was celebrating Canada's one-hundredth birthday with a variety of activities and those activities involved such things as plays, dances and Winnipeg's Pan American Games. I can't recall how many museums I visited that year, but there were lots of them.

In order for me to get to know where the historical places were, including the museums, as well, I would catch a tour bus outside the hotels where I was staying. If memory serves me, correctly, the guided tour bus trips back in 1967 cost me no more than $2.00 per tour. Each bus I took would take me and the other passengers to the historical sites and we would then exit the bus and go and see whatever exhibits there were at each location.

After a short period of time, which allowed the passengers to study each area, we would return to the bus and the tour would continue on. When each tour was finished, we returned to the hotel.

The very next day, I would walk to the places we visited on the guided tour bus trip because I realized that the historical places we saw on the bus trips were located very close to the hotel. So I took lots of guided tour bus trips in that year of 1967 and did lots of walking as well as going to the numerous historical sites. Each bus trip, taken by me, all across Canada seemed to not have travelled that far from the hotels where I stayed at, so it was very possible for me to pack lots of Canadian history into my life by taking these bus tours.

Well, the summer of 1967, quickly came to an end and I was back in Edmonton ready to start my second year of teaching. Each year, after

1967, the two months of summer holidays would, of course, always come. During these summer months, I continued with my travelling way of life. In 1968, I went to see the pyramids of Mexico and learned about Mexican history. Then in 1970, my sister, Lila, and I went to Expo in Osaka, Japan, and, also, we had the opportunity to visit Taiwan and Hong Kong on that occasion. The Japan trip showed me how kind the Japanese were. They loved to have their picture taken and they seemed to always be smiling in the pictures that I took. Also, in Tokyo, I had the opportunity to eat spaghetti with chopsticks. That was an interesting adventure when I tried to wrap the spaghetti around the chopsticks so that I could get some of it into my mouth. Have you ever tried to wrap spaghetti around chopsticks? If you haven't, try it someday just for the fun of it!

For me, the Japanese trip allows me to think back to the time, when a group of us were eating in a restaurant. When we had finished our meal, we wanted to go to a certain place for some evening entertainment. We, however, had no idea as to how to get to the place. After paying for our meals, we then asked the cashier for directions. He tried to give us the directions but we just weren't able to follow those directions which were given. The cashier then went to one of the customers and, to this day, I have no idea if the cashier knew the customer. Anyway, the customer got out of his chair and stood by the door and then motioned us to follow him. The customer left the restaurant and we followed him, walking at times and running at other times until he got us to our destination. It was one of those times, in my life, that will stick with me forever.

Before the Japanese trip, a teachers' group, out of Ottawa, in 1969, advertised an Easter Holiday tour of the Soviet Union for a ten-day period. I jumped at the opportunity to take this trip because the price of the trip, under $1000, included airfare, accommodations and food which was extremely reasonable and the trip meant that I could further enhance my historical knowledge.

I will never regret taking any of these holiday trips in my early days when I had the enthusiasm to learn and the good health that allowed me to enjoy these time periods. These were all enjoyable trips and the prices for these early holidays were nothing short of being tremendously cheap and in comparison with today's prices would put the prices for the present-day travel to shame. Further travels during the years ahead would take me to Hawaii on several different occasions.

There was always enjoyment to these trips that I took over those years. The year, 1977, however came along and I took a trip I really hesitated in taking. It was the trip to Washington, D.C. My sister, Emily, was hospitalized at the time with breast cancer. While in Washington, I would stay at Emily's apartment which was located just across the street from the infamous Watergate building—so needless to say, I went to the Watergate building which had, in those days, several businesses in it on the lower floor. The building even had a Safeway store in it where I did some grocery shopping.

Emily's friends, from her workplace, at the World Bank, would offer all kinds of extended hands to ensure that my visit to Washington was as enjoyable as it could possibly be even though Emily was in the hospital for the whole time period that I was there. Later on, I returned to Edmonton and reported on Emily's health to my siblings. At times, while I was telling my siblings about Emily's health, I broke down and it was impossible for me to prevent tears from running down my face. My sister, Emily, would, eventually, be brought to Edmonton by my brothers Alex and Teddy, who went to Washington with the specific task of bringing her to Edmonton where she would spend the final days of her life. Emily passed away at the age of 55 in 1978. She was buried alongside of our Mother, Mary, in the Beechmount Cemetery.

When Dad was told that Emily had passed away, I remember that he started to cry while he sat in his chair and said the following words, "A father should pass away before any of his children." For some unknown reason, I had the responsibility of picking out Emily's gravestone and my brother, Mickey, would get an employee of his, Kemal Baghdady, to work on the necessary information in the Arabic language for her gravestone. As other family members passed away, I would continue to hold the responsibility of acquiring most of the gravestones when needed and, in addition, for a number of my siblings, I would give the eulogy at their funeral service.

After Emily had died, Dad was the next family member to pass away. He would live to the grand old age of ninety-seven and passed away on November 3rd, 1979. Dad had prostate cancer and near the end of his life, he would be hospitalized for his final days. It wouldn't be the cancer, however, that ended his life and as in so many other cases, when a person's life comes to an end, it is often the heart that fails. Dad passed away from heart failure in his last year of life.

I remember clearly the night when Dad died. The rains came pouring down for a number of minutes. Those heavy rains, in my way of thinking, meant that the heavens had opened up that night in order to allow Dad to go to his final resting place away from Earth.

After Dad's funeral, it took a while for Lila's life, along with my own life, as well, to return to normal. Lila would work her heart out at the wholesale and I continued on with my teaching career.

There are all kinds of things that I can say about my teaching years, other than what I mentioned earlier on in my writing. There were a number of ups and downs in my teaching years, but I can say with great pride that I had many more ups than downs. All of my years of teaching were in the elementary grades. I taught every subject, except for music, during those teaching years. For several years, I co-ordinated the school patrol program and I ran the yearly track meet for numerous years, as well. I took pride in wanting my students to bring out the best that they could give towards their learning so that they could help lead themselves onto a path of success. I never gave up on any student because, deep down, I knew that, somehow, I could help each and everyone of them. During my teaching career, I really enjoyed helping the weaker academic students who got down on themselves a lot, at times. I encouraged a number of my students to change their way of thinking to a more positive manner and this made it possible for them to become better students. I am not going to say that I was successful with all of the students I taught, but I am willing to say that I, honestly, put much time and effort into the lives of my students in order to make them as successful as possible.

In addition to my teaching career, I started to become, actively, involved in a number of organizations. I became President of the Edmonton Multicultural Society, a society which promoted multiculturalism where each ethnic group across Canada and, especially, in the Edmonton area was well-respected and where we could learn from each other the values that each group could share with others.

Another group that I was a member of was the Alberta Heritage Council which was an Alberta-wide government sponsored organization and promoted the issues of multiculturalism on several different occasions throughout the year. This council had some teeth to it because of its backing by the Alberta government. I, also, helped to start a club known as the Canadian Arab Friendship Association. In the beginning years of this Club, starting in 1965, the Club had many successful events. Each year, we would put on a grand party where we invited a number of dignitaries. This grand party's name in Arabic was called the Haflah.

The Association would, also, spend time over the years putting on conferences which dealt with the present-day issues in those days. Unfortunately, some members decided to take over the organization indicating that they were not pleased with the way things were being run. This group would win the election that took place in that year and then they started to run the organization according to the desires they had. The Canadian Arab Friendship Association continues to exist today, but, in my opinion, it has wandered away from its original mandate as set out in the Club's constitution.

I, also, became a founding member of the Canadian Arab Professional and Business Club. This Club would exist for a number of years, but as time went on, the members, for whatever reason or reasons gave up on the Club and it, gradually, died a slow death. A third organization that I became a part of was the Arabic Language Advisory Council Society and this organization was started to help out the Arabic-English Bilingual Program which, in 1982, was housed within the Edmonton Public School System. Although this society would, eventually, fade away, I did have the opportunity to work with Soraya Zaki Hafez on trying to ensure that the Arabic Language Advisory Council Society would be a strong advocate of promoting the Arabic-English Bilingual Program within the public school system.

Soraya was the first teacher in the Edmonton Public School Board's Arabic-English Bilingual Program and she would devote many hours on strengthening the program during its early years. In addition, Soraya would spend a number of years as a part-time curriculum writer for the Arabic-English Bilingual Program. Because of the effort, Soraya put forward in her curriculum writing position, future teachers in the program would have a lot of information to work with as they taught their way through the academic subjects the students were required to take. Her curriculum writing position would take Soraya to countries such as Jordan and Egypt where she purchased educational books she thought would be needed by the students in Edmonton in order to help them learn a lot about the Arab world as well as the Arabic language.

When the Arabic-English Bilingual Program began, it was started in the basement of the Al Rashid Mosque which is part of the Canadian Islamic Centre. After a few years, the parent group associated with the Bilingual program decided to approach the Edmonton Public School Board and then asked the Board if the Arabic-English Bilingual Program could become a program housed within the Edmonton Public School System. After some negotiations, Edmonton Public agreed to take in the Arabic-English Bilingual Program. So the Program moved from the Al Rashid Mosque to Glengarry School. Soraya Hafez would now have the honour of becoming known as the first Arabic-English teacher in an Arabic-English Bilingual Program in all of Canada where the Arabic-English Bilingual Program would be taught as part of the daily curriculum in a Canadian school system during the regular school hours. It should, also, be noted that other Canadian school systems, in some parts of Canada, were teaching some form of an Arabic-English Bilingual Program, but these school systems were teaching their programs outside of the regular school hours. After a while, in Edmonton, a second elementary school would open with an Arabic-English Bilingual Program on its premises. A Junior High School in the following year would, also, open where that school housed the Arabic-English Bilingual Program.

Today, new schools continue to open within the Edmonton Public School System with the Arabic-English Bilingual Program being part of some of those educational institutions.

Dad, you only met Soraya on a few occasions when special activities were being held and there were those times when you and I attended those gatherings. In time, Soraya and her husband, would divorce and after that divorce took place, Soraya and I would start having a romantic relationship with each other and by 1988, the two of us talked about getting married and that is, exactly, what we did. Unfortunately, you were not living at this time in order to witness what was taking place.

On July 9th, 1988, Soraya and I took our wedding vows. That summer, we would spend our honeymoon in Cairo, Egypt where I got to know Soraya's family members. On the other hand, Soraya got to know our family members. Many of my sisters and brothers were all present at the wedding. It was a very happy occasion for Soraya and myself.

Dad, it took a long time for me to get married and one of the reasons for the late marriage was that my sister, Lila, and myself, devoted a lot of our lives looking after you. I want you to know that both Lila and I, in no way, ever regret spending that time with you, but I do feel sorry that Lila never married. She has been too much of a caring person to remain single all of her life.

After our marriage, Soraya and I would spend a lot of time travelling to numerous parts of the world. We went to several locations within Canada, visited Syria, Jordan and went to Egypt on several different occasions. In the year 2000, Dad, Soraya and I went to Lebanon and visited Lala, the village where you were born. In Lala, we met a lot of our relatives and from the outside we even saw the house you were born in. Unfortunately, the relatives who lived in the house at that time didn't invite us into the home of your birth. I assume they had a reason or reasons for behaving the way they did. Eventhough, I was disappointed on not seeing the inside of your birth house, I must admit that Soraya and I both loved our visit to Lebanon and, especially, to the village of Lala. These are days that I can never forget because for most of those days there are a lot of untold stories which have to be kept for some other time.

Today, Dad, I am walking alone along several of the paths we once travelled together. As I walk alone, I still think of you, Pop, walking beside me. I am constantly recalling many of the stories you told me and they continue to circulate in my head as I continue on with those walks.

I realize that certain days can never come back to life, for me, but I, also, know that many of those days will live within me forever.

I want you to know, Dad, that life for Soraya and myself, over many years was very good, but the last several years have been kind of tough. Over these years, we have lost a lot of family members and friends. Only four of our family, as I said earlier, are still living. These four are Lila, Sine, Jimmy and myself. On the other hand, a lot of our nieces and nephews have married and they now have a number of children of their own and many of them continue to live here in Edmonton. I cannot say for certain how much these younger members know about our family's history, but if they read this book, they, definitely, will be able to enhance their knowledge of the family, you and Mom started over one hundred years ago. Let's hope that their future interests will partially lie in wanting to know more about their many relatives.

Dad at this time, I am very pleased to tell you that my wife, Soraya, received a very great honour on May 8th, 2018. On that day, the Edmonton Public School Board announced that a brand new school, that is scheduled to open in September of the year 2020 will be named after Soraya and this school will be called the Soraya Hafez School. The school is an elementary school and will have grades going from Kindergarten to Grade Six. In my mind, there is no doubt, whatsoever, that Soraya is very deserving of this honour by having a school named after her.

With this good news, I now, unfortunately, have to mention some sad news about Soraya. In July of 2015, Soraya suffered two strokes. One of the two strokes left her paralyzed on the right side and took her ability to speak, from her, at the same time. I had a speech specialist work with Soraya, but her ability to speak never came back up to this time. Hopefully, some day, her speech will return in the time period ahead of us. Needless, to say, Dad, I, honestly, believe in miracles taking place.

After Soraya had her strokes, she stayed at the University Hospital for several weeks. As the weeks went by, the doctors said that there wasn't anything more that could be done for her. I was told by the doctor, who was looking after her, that Soraya would have to go to an extended care facility. I then had talks with the social workers at the University Hospital and they gave me suggestions as to where Soraya could be placed. I discussed these suggestions with her two grown children from her first marriage. After the discussions took place, the two children felt that it would be best to place her in an extended care facility near where they lived because they felt it would be possible for them and their families to visit Soraya a fair amount. At this time, however, I felt that they gave little, if any thoughts, about my feelings when it came to choosing a location for her to live at.

I remember, in my conversations with the social workers that they told me that in cases, like Soraya's situation, the spouse is usually the one who will devote more of his or her time in the extended care facility as time goes on. Furthermore, the social workers said that people, other than the spouse, always say that they will be around with the ill person—in this case their mother and their grandmother. Soraya treated her children and grandchildren with a royal-like treatment when she was in good health. There is no doubt in my mind, that the social workers were very accurate in the information they gave me.

Before Soraya had her strokes, she and I went to a lawyer. At that meeting with the lawyer, both Soraya and myself made each other's his/her Power of Attorney. We would now be given the right to act on behalf of the other person for situations that might arise in our lives. This Power of Attorney that I now had meant that I would care for Soraya and Soraya would care for me if and when any health situations arose.

I then used my Power of Attorney authority and decided to move Soraya to an extended care facility near where the two of us have our house. Although the daughter and son seemed not to be pleased with my decision to move Soraya to the General Hospital Extended Case Facility, am I ever glad that I made this decision. This extended care centre is only about ten minutes away from where our home is. In fact our home is on the same street where our family lived years ago. Our own family moved out of that family home, in the area known as Rossdale, around 1950.

Soraya's daughter was, extremely, upset with me for placing Soraya where I did. The daughter's behavior became very unkind towards me, after Soraya was placed in the extended care centre. She would start doing all kinds of ridiculous and silly things just to irritate me. At one point she said that she would not talk to me again if Soraya stayed at the extended care centre I placed her in. The daughter considered this place to be unsuitable for Soraya. I paid very little attention to her concerns at this time.

When Soraya and I were awarded with a prize for peace, I placed the information on the Bulletin Board in Soraya's room and the daughter took it down and probably threw it away. I never saw that particular piece of information again. Luckily, I had some other copies about this award and I put another copy on the Bulletin Board. Once again, the daughter took it down. Unfortunately, because of the daughter's uncalled for behavior, I decided to not put the information up again on the Bulletin Board. It is really sad that I caved in to the daughter's ridiculous and extremely childish behavior.

Looking back on my decision to place Soraya close to where we live, in a facility that has a good reputation, as well, I believe that I definitely, made the right decision for Soraya. Over the number of months that Soraya has been in the extended care centre, I have visited her everyday for anywhere from six to nine hours on weekends and anywhere from eight to ten hours on weekdays. In the beginning, Soraya's children shared in coming on each of the seven days of the week. However, for whatever reason or reasons, they started to cut back on the hours they would come and visit Soraya. The grandchildren, also, have shown that they are coming a lot less often than they should, in my opinion. Some of the granddaughters, also, have shown some disrespect for me as well. No matter what, Dad, I have learned to accept their behavior and I can live with the situation they have provided me with. Also, Dad, I am disappointed in the numerous friends that Soraya and I once had. Soraya would often invite many of the friends to the various gatherings we had at our house. These friends were there for us in the beginning when Soraya had the strokes, but, in time, they, also, became the so-called friends who disappeared as time went on.

Today, my wife, Soraya, continues to be at the extended care centre. Each day she is fed protein through a tube leading into her stomach area. She is fed four times each day using the tube. I will never forget that when Soraya first had her strokes, it appeared that she was going to die. Soraya, however, seemed to have had a great desire to live which she continues to do at this time. Her awareness of what is happening around her seems to be quite good. I will continue to come and be with Soraya, with the hope, that each time I visit her, that I am providing her with some comfort.

At this time, Pop, I, honestly, don't know what life has in store for us, but I do know that I, along with Soraya, will live the rest of our lives to the fullest extent possible.

Dad, back in 1994, my brother Sine, Soraya and myself all retired from the teaching profession. The Edmonton Public Schools held a Retirement Banquet for those teachers who were leaving the profession. A booklet was put out that year which honoured the retiring teachers. The booklet had some information about the retiring teachers. The information about Sine has already been given when I told something about Sine earlier in my writing of this book.

Now, I want to let you know what they said about Soraya and myself in that 1994 Retirement Banquet book. First of all, here is what they said about Soraya.

"Soraya was a pioneer in making the Arabic language available to children. For the past eleven years, she taught at Glengarry, Malmo and Queen Elizabeth schools. She is a dedicated and committed teacher who is appreciated for her leadership in cultural activities. Students, staff, and parents valued her commitment to the integration of Arabic students into the total program of the school.

Throughout her career, Soraya has demonstrated personal initiative and commitment to the teaching profession through significant involvement in professional development activities with the district, Alberta Education and the University of Alberta in the training of new teachers. Soraya has been acknowledged for her expertise in Arabic programming, curriculum writing and willingness to share her knowledge with others.

As Soraya looks forward to her retirement, she will be missed for her keen sense of humour and the rapport she established with students, staff, and the community."

Finally, Dad, this is what the banquet book said about me. "As a teacher at Laurier Heights, Scott Robertson, Lynnwood and Westglen schools, Richard has provided a valuable service for twenty-seven years.

Throughout his teaching career, Richard's commitment and dedication to the profession has been exemplary and evident through his participation in professional development activities at the school and the district, the Alberta Teachers' Association and the Alberta Association for Multicultural Education.

He is known as a teacher who sets high standards for himself and his students and ensured that these standards were met. As a co-operative staff member, he is always willing to support and assist with the total school program. Richard's extensive work organizing the fiftieth anniversary at Westglen was particularly appreciated.

As Richard looks forward to his retirement, change of career and new food catering business, he will be remembered for his many contributions and missed for his great sense of humour".

Dad, both you and I have told a lot of stories where at one point, we walked along a path together and in our walking ventures, we recalled so many interesting things that happened in both of our lives. The journey, we undertook, led us to tell all kinds of stories. We told stories to each other, and these stories were full of much happiness, at times, but at other times the stories brought sadness into our lives. As some stories were being told, tears would flow from our eyes. You and I both had numerous relatives and friends who played a pretty big part in our lives and these relatives and friends allowed us to understand what true friendship meant to you, me and our family.

Dad, I will continue to walk the paths we followed when you and I told those stories to each other. My love for you and Mom, along with my love for my brothers, sisters and friends, as well as my love for my wife, Soraya, will always be there.

In closing, Dad, I want you to know that I wouldn't change the lives we have led, in anyway at all. May God bless you, Mom, our family and, as well, our many dear friends!

Remembering Stories Through Pictures

Through the World of Pictures, I now bring my story to an end. So walk with me, my friends, as you look at the faces and the activities that made it possible for my father and me to walk the paths that brought our stories to life.

Ahmed Ali Awid

My Dad,
Ahmed Ali Awid

Nephew, Kasim Amery,
Dad and nephew,
Sid Amery

*Mom and Dad on the front steps
of the new house*

*Grandfather (Mom's dad)
and Emily*

Grandfather

*Left: Grandfather (Mom's Dad)
Right: Uncle Pete
Others in picture are unknown*

Back: Dad, Mom
Front: Richard, Lila

Mom, Richard (holding Kelp), Lila, Kemal

Unknown relative, Lila, Mom,
Grandfather

Dad, Emily, Alex Amery
on Dad's way to Mecca

Dad visited by Arab Business People
from Eastern Canada

Dad's Passport Picture

Mom, Emily, Dad

Richard and Mickey

Lily

Lila

Sine's wife, Verna, June and Alex's daughter, Bonnie, June, Alex's wife

Lila is dressed for Klondike days

Minnie, Zina, Evelyn, Lily

Mona Loftson (nee AWID)

February 22, 1921 - October 11, 2000

Emily in 1946

Zina

Karen, Joel, Lily, Joe

*Mona, Barney, Cherlene,
Carla, David*

Emily, Mona, Zina

Mona, Mickey, Emily

*Zina, Mona, Lily,
Richard and Kelp*

Lily, husband, Joe and Emily

Mona

Lily

Sister Mona, ready for a wedding

The new house that Mickey and
Alex built for the family

My mother, Mary, Emily, my sister
and my father, Ahmed Awid

Dad and Mom

Dad with two of his grandchildren

Dad and Mom

Kemal, Dad, Lila, Mom, Richard

Alex Awid

Mickey Awid

Eddie Awid

Ted Awid

Eddie Awid
1933 - 2006

My sister, Zina and brother, Ted

Mickey, Dad, Sine

Awid family members enjoying a family get together
Sine is pictured to my left

Kemal doing some acting

Richard

Mona, Jim,
Gwen

*Mickey, Lila holding
pet dog, Kelp, Richard*

*Left to right:
Jim, Sine, Teddy, Eddie*

Mickey and Evelyn

Teddy and wife, Marianne

Kemal doing some babysitting

Zina and pet
dog, Kelp

Emily in her
office at the
World Bank

Emily with
one of her
boyfriends

Zina enjoying
winter

Ready for Klondike Days
Back: Mickey, Evelyn
Front: Linda, Cindy

Evelyn, Dad, Mickey

Left to Right:
Donald, Jeff, Evelyn, Dad,
Mohammed Amery, Mickey

Santa pays Dad a visit

Dad and Patty - A birthday
celebration

Head stone for Jim Darwish located in Muslim section of Beechmount Cemetery, Edmonton

Alex Amery and Dad

*Ali Tarrabin
accompanied Dad
when coming to Canada*

Our cousin, Frank Almer

*Members of Canada's first Mosque built in Edmonton, Alberta in 1938.
Picture taken around 1940. In the top row, second from left, is Dad*

Aunt Vera, uncle Sam Jamha

Alex Darwish (1940)

Mike Tarrabain

Lila Tarrabain

Najeebie Houssian

Frank Amery

Mahmoud Tarrabain

Peter Baker

Alex and Khadija Amerey

Ameen King Ganam

Richard, the Teacher

Mom in a relaxing position

Ahmed Ali Awid and Sam Jamha

Richard in his younger days

*Imam Shibley, Soraya, Saleem Ganam
and Richard taking wedding vows,
July 9, 1988*

*Richard and Soraya enjoying
a night out*

*Soraya and Richard participating
in Arab function*

Richard and Soraya in Cairo

Soraya and son, Tariq

*Soraya Hafez and two
of her students*

Soraya and Richard

Dr. Lila Fahlman

Richard, the young Teacher

Richard during his teaching years

Nature nut was inspired by teacher

Barbara Grinder

When asked who his favourite teacher was when he was a child attending school in Alberta, renowned scientist, writer and broadcaster John Acorn replied, "That's easy—my Grade 5 teacher, Richard Awid."

A student at Laurier Heights School, in Edmonton, for nine years, Acorn says that Awid was his first male teacher. "But that's not what made him memorable. He was the first teacher I had who stood up for me when other kids razzed me about looking at bugs and spiders. He legitimized my interest and showed the kids that insects really were neat things to study. He did so much for my self-confidence."

Acorn's childhood interest in insects and arachnids led to a master's degree in entomology from the University of Alberta and a long career in the media fostering an interest in natural history in readers and viewers.

"The other thing I remember about Mr. Awid—and maybe it's the most important thing about him—was that he was the first person to teach us that it was important to listen to other people's opinions. For me, that was the right time to learn that message, and it's something I've never forgotten," he recalls.

Acorn admits that he wasn't always the easiest student to have around but says that Awid wasn't an easy teacher, either: "I

John Acorn and his Grade 5 teacher, Richard Awid

Mr. Awid was the first teacher I had who stood up for me when other kids razzed me about looking at bugs and spiders. He legitimized my interest and showed the kids that insects really were neat things to study. He did so much for my self-confidence."

—John Acorn

remember one time I was spinning a ruler around the tip of a pen, through one of those little holes in the ruler. Mr. Awid finally got fed up with my being disruptive and had me stay after class and keep spinning that ruler. I was only allowed to stop when the tip of the pen broke from all the friction."

Awid was active in Edmonton's Muslim community; he wrote several books about its history and was a researcher and keynote speaker on the Arab community in Alberta.

"There's a growing xenophobia about people from other cultures in Canada," Acorn says. "It scares me and it reminds me of Mr. Awid's lesson about respecting other people's opinions.

I think it's a lesson we all need to remember."

John Acorn is a scientist, writer and broadcaster. He currently teaches in the Department of Renewable Resources at the University of Alberta. He is the host and creator of the TV program "Acorn, the Nature Nut," a 92-episode series that aired on the Discovery Channel.

Soraya and Richard